Running
the Race with God

366 Inspiring Daily Devotionals for Victorious Christian Living

THEMBEKILE MAYAYISE

WESTBOW
PRESS
A DIVISION OF THOMAS NELSON

WestBow Press books may be ordered through booksellers or by contacting:

WestBow Press
A Division of Thomas Nelson
1663 Liberty Drive
Bloomington, IN 47403
www.westbowpress.com
1-(866) 928-1240

Because of the dynamic nature of the Internet, any web addresses or links contained in this book may have changed since publication and may no longer be valid. The views expressed in this work are solely those of the author and do not necessarily reflect the views of the publisher, and the publisher hereby disclaims any responsibility for them.

Any people depicted in stock imagery provided by Thinkstock are models, and such images are being used for illustrative purposes only.

Certain stock imagery © Thinkstock.

ISBN: 978-1-4497-3521-0 (sc)
ISBN: 978-1-4497-3522-7 (hbk)
ISBN: 978-1-4497-3520-3 (e)

Library of Congress Control Number: 2011963024

Printed in the United States of America

WestBow Press rev. date: 1/09/2012

Contents

About the Author

Thembekile Mayayise is a born-again Christian and a member of the Evangelical Presbyterian Church in South Africa. Ever since she gave her life to Jesus at the age of sixteen, she has enjoyed and nurtured her relationship with Jesus. She is passionate about the things of God and serving Him. She often teaches God's Word in church group gatherings and God has used her to encourage and motivate other believers. She holds a master's degree in Information Technology from the University of Pretoria and is married with two kids.

Acknowledgments

I thank God Almighty for the inspiration and the strength He gave to write this book. It has been a great and interesting journey.

I would like to thank my family, particularly my husband and kids for giving me the space to work on this book. My friends have immensely supported me throughout this project and I would like to thank them for their advice and help. My mother has taught me great lessons in life such as how to persevere in the most trying times and how to have faith in God. I would like to thank her for having been such a great teacher.

Lastly, I would like to thank my Reverend and all the members of my church, the Evangelical Presbyterian, Braamfontein, in South Africa, for speaking life over my sharing of the Gospel of Jesus. My church has been a great source of motivation and encouragement during my spiritual journey. May God bless you always.

Bible Translations

This book consists of twelve themed chapters that represent the twelve months of the year. The scriptures that have been used are from various Bible translations: the New Living Translation (NLT), New International Version (NIV), English Standard Version (ESV), King James Version (KJV), New American Standard Bible/Version (NASV), American Standard Version (ASV), American King James Version (AKJV), International Standard Version (ISV), and the World English Bible (WEB).

Chapter 1

Make God's Kingdom
a Priority in Your Life

1 January

"Seek the Kingdom of God above all else, and live righteously, and he will give you everything you need" (Matthew. 6:33, NLT).

Today you may be starting a new season in your life—a new month, a new year, a new relationship, or a new job or school. As you begin, I urge you to start that new season in your life by seeking the Kingdom of God first, to live in righteousness, and to see the promise of God manifest in your life. Sometimes we go through delays in our lives; at times, we don't achieve any breakthroughs because we have set our minds on things that do not align with God's will for our lives.

God's Kingdom is of utmost importance because, just as in a worldly kingdom where the king presides, rules and standards are defined and adhered. In God's Kingdom, He gives instructions and reveals His secrets. When you seek the Kingdom of God, you will be consumed by working only on things that will matter to God's Kingdom. When you have a challenging job and you can't make sense of where you should focus, seek God's Kingdom and be filled with God's understanding. Then watch everything being added unto you.

You may have tried different things in life, such as trusting in your own abilities and strength—and they could have yielded results in certain aspects of your life—but you may not be fulfilled. You may have ventured into business, hoping to become rich one day. You could be rich now—but not fulfilled—because you have not sought the right thing, which God expects you to seek first. God loves you and He wants you to seek first His Kingdom and live a righteous life. The promise God gives us is that everything else will be added unto us.

Make God's Kingdom a priority in your life and live a righteous life because God's Kingdom goes hand in hand with righteous living. When you invest time in God's Word and prayer and spending time with God, everything you need will be added unto you. After all, God has everything that you need. Proverbs 8:18 says, "With me are riches and honour, enduring wealth and prosperity."

Prayer of the Day

Dear Father, I repent of my sins for I know that I have been giving priority to other things and neglecting the things of your Kingdom. I yield my whole being to serve you and to receive your Kingdom into my life, giving it a priority. Help me to live for you, in Jesus's name. Amen.

2 January

"God blesses those who are persecuted for doing right, for the Kingdom of Heaven is theirs" (Matthew. 5:10, NLT).

Prayer Point

Sometimes we allow the world to dictate how we should behave as Christians instead of looking at the Word of God to show us the way of living a righteous life. We need to live a life as Christians that will stand out—no matter which country or family we come from.

As you pray today, ask God to help you to spiritually locate fellow Christians by faith through prayer. They may live in different parts of the world and may be persecuted for Jesus Christ's sake. Pray that they may persevere in faith and continue doing what is good so that they may inherit the Kingdom of God.

Pray that the Spirit of God within you leads you into doing things the godly way, regardless of what the world dictates. Let the Holy Spirit fill you with the love, patience, and joy for the Kingdom of God and make you patient for God's Kingdom.

3 January

"So if you ignore the least commandment and teach others to do the same, you will be called the least in the Kingdom of Heaven. But anyone who obeys God's laws and teaches them will be called great in the Kingdom of Heaven" (Matthew. 5:19, NLT).

Prayer Point

As His children, God expects us to respect His Word and to be doers of His Word. His Word is a vital way for God to guide us and to lead us into righteous living. Every part of God's Word is important and should be shared with equal emphasis and importance.

Pray that God gives you the wisdom to share His Word with others in a manner that will be pleasing to Him and will bring glory to Him. Ask God to help you lead an exemplary life before others, a life that demonstrates true obedience to God.

Allow the power of God through the Holy Spirit to transform your actions to be obedient to God's laws. In this way, other people can be transformed into godly life through you. Allow the Holy Spirit to help you meditate on God's commands—that you may live righteously.

4 January

"You can enter God's Kingdom only through the narrow gate. The highway to hell is broad, and its gate is wide for the many who choose that way" (Matthew. 7:13, NLT).

Prayer Point

The world we live in is so full of attractions that consume us and take a lot of our time and attention. As children of God, we need to use our God-given wisdom to do the things that will make it possible for us to enter God's Kingdom. We need to pray even when none of us seems to feel like praying. We need to fast when the world feels it's the best season to buy food and indulge.

Pray for guidance that you may serve God's Kingdom as much as you can, so that you don't fall into temptation and do things that will lead you to sin. Seek to do the things that are less popular to the world, but valuable in God's Kingdom. Long to hear from God and what He wants you to do for Him.

Pray for all those friends and family members whom you know have chosen to travel the highway to hell, asking God that they may repent today, so that their life may be preserved for eternity. Pray for yourself, that you may choose the life that will lead you to eternity through Christ.

5 January

"But if I am casting out demons by the Spirit of God, then the Kingdom of God has arrived among you" (Matthew. 12:28, NLT).

Prayer Point

When the Lord Jesus was on earth, He performed many miracles, such as healing the sick and casting out evil spirits. He cast out demons by the power of God. As children of God, we also possess that power through our faith in Him. A sign that God's Kingdom is in us appears when we do the things that Christ did during His ministry.

As you devote time to prayer today, draw nearer to God with a repenting heart. Ask God to forgive you for all your sins. Pray for God's Spirit to reveal to you the gifts with which He has blessed you, so that you can start using those gifts for His Kingdom. Be obedient to His Word and stand in faith so that whatever Gift He reveals, you will use it with love and not out of selfish ambition, giving evidence of God's Kingdom.

Remember that, in order for God's Kingdom to dwell within you, your life should be one of pursuing God's Kingdom so that you live in the ways God expects of you.

6 January

"I'll say it again—it is easier for a camel to go through the eye of a needle than for a rich person to enter the Kingdom of God!" (Matthew. 19:24, NLT).

Prayer Point

It is good for us to be blessed and to have financial prosperity. God expects us to live a good life—a life that demonstrates abundance and not lack—because lack does not describe who God is. As we enjoy the blessings with which God has blessed us, we ought to remember that our source of prosperity is God. He is always worthy of glory.

Wealth and material belongings do not define your relationship with God. When wealth takes priority over God, it becomes impossible for you to enter God's Kingdom.

I invite you to pray for the removal of all the things in your life that are making you pay less attention to the things of God and could prevent you from entering God's Kingdom. Pray that you see spending eternity with God as the most important focus, rather than chasing after worldly riches, which only bears significance during our temporary stay on earth.

7 January

"I tell you, the Kingdom of God will be taken away from you and given to a nation that will produce the proper fruit" (Matthew. 21:43, NLT).

Prayer Point

The Kingdom of God is like a seed that, when planted in good soil and given proper care, produces abundant fruit in due season. In order not to lose the Kingdom of God, we must take care of it until it yields fruits, so that we can continue living together as a nation that bears good fruits.

As you pray today, allow the Holy Spirit in you to transform your mind so that you may bear the proper fruit, to which our Lord Jesus refers. Pray that God helps you to live a life that cultivates the seed planted within you, so that you may start bearing fruit for God's glory.

Pray for your family and people in different ministries—especially those who have been stagnant in their service. Pray that God resurrects their faith and restores His Kingdom in their lives so that they can start bearing fruit.

8 January

"Work hard to enter the narrow door to God's Kingdom, for many will try to enter but will fail" (Luke 13:24, NLT).

Imagine soccer fans going to watch two very popular soccer teams play in a stadium. You would find that almost every supporter of those teams would be in a rush for the game. As many people fight to enter the stadium, only a few people can go through at a time because the gate becomes more and more narrow. In essence, the supporters would need to work very hard to enter the narrow gate that leads to the stadium. It takes patience and sometimes a bit of a physical push to force your way through. Another issue to consider is that even those supporters with valid tickets for entry; may also need to exercise a bit of patience when they enter the stadium. In certain countries, law prohibits harmful substances or weapons inside the stadium.

This scenario is similar to when we try to enter the Kingdom of God. The door to the Kingdom is narrow and anyone who does not have the patience and is not willing to work hard and push their way into the Kingdom would fail. Worldly possessions often make people feel important and successful, but the Bible cautions us that these worldly attachments may make it harder for rich people to enter the Kingdom of God (Luke 18:24).

Entering the Kingdom of God may also require letting go of certain habits (envy, hatred, bitterness, pride, and resentment) because these attributes do not conform to the Kingdom standards.

As you aim to enter the Kingdom of God, may God cleanse your spirit of any hatred and resentment and help you to live a life that is righteous so that you may enter the narrow door with ease.

Prayer of the Day

Father God, when I do things that are full of temporary pleasure, always have your way to remind me in the manner that will make me realize it is you talking to me, so that I may start working hard and do the things that are important and necessary to your kingdom. Give me the ability to persevere in areas where other people would find it difficult to persevere. Help me to get rid of the chains that seem physically unbreakable so that I may walk in your presence. In Jesus's name, I thank you. Amen.

9 January

"The Kingdom of God is like a farmer who scatters seed on the ground" (Mark 4:26, NLT).

Prayer Point

Jesus used different parables to help us understand more about the Kingdom of God. The Kingdom of God is about receiving it and being able to produce the fruit that will be the result of the Kingdom.

As you pray today, ask God to nurture the Word that has been planted in you through the messages that you have heard and the scriptures you have read. There is a specific fruit that God expects you to bear through the seed that was planted in you. Pray that God transforms you so that you can fulfill the call that God has predestined for you.

Pray that God remove any obstacle that is preventing you from living the life that adheres to the Kingdom's principles. Seek God's face for wisdom, guidance, and revelations into living the life of purpose that God has given you.

10 January

"Jesus went on to say, 'I tell you the truth, some standing here right now will not die before they see the Kingdom of God arrive in great power!'" (Mark 9:1, NLT).

Prayer Point

The evidence that the Kingdom of God has arrived in great power is in the demonstration of God's power (performing miracles, casting out demons, and healing the sick). There are people who have died without realizing God's power upon their lives in greatness.

Pray that God leads you into the life of awareness of His presence and working that you may start seeing mysteries of His Kingdom. Pray for perseverance in all circumstances that you do not pass this world without having experienced God's Kingdom in fullness.

Have a special prayer for your friends or family members who have not accepted Lord Jesus that the Kingdom of God gets revealed in them through great power so that the power of God takes them by surprise and they will be drawn to it by God's grace.

11 January

"And if your eye causes you to sin, gouge it out. It's better to enter the Kingdom of God with only one eye than to have two eyes and be thrown into hell" (Mark 9:47, NLT).

Prayer Point

During our time on earth, we may stumble in different areas and only manage to get up through the help of God. Pray that God helps you to stop sinning in areas where you know you are struggling because God expects us to be righteous in all areas of our lives and to strive for righteousness in all that we do. Refuse to accommodate sins because sin will never accommodate your salvation; sin leads to death.

Pray for the yoke to be broken of spiritual paralysis that is causing stagnation and hindering you from serving God with all your heart. Let all people of bad influence out of your life; stick to people who nurture a godly walk and encourage you to live a righteous life.

Pray for God to guard your heart and for all your actions to be the actions that will be in full support of working for God's Kingdom.

12 January

"When Jesus saw what was happening, He was angry with his disciples. He said to them, "Let the children come to me. Don't stop them! For the Kingdom of God belongs to those who are like these children" (Mark 10:14, NLT).

Prayer Point

Children are loved by God and Lord Jesus because of how children are. Children are honest, they seldom pretend, they often believe what their parents say, and they tend to take things at face value. Another attribute of children is their innocence; they don't act up to be mature and they often don't mind a lot of things that adults are concerned about. When a parent says something for the first time to a child, they are likely to believe their parents. When they become older, they may start questioning their parents.

Our faith in God requires us to ask fewer questions about why certain things happen the way they do and trying to challenge God's thinking. Our faith in God requires us to take His Word for it, believing that He knows best.

As you pray today, ask that God helps you to have a childlike attitude and be humble that He may draw closer to you. Pray that He may increase your insight in the understanding of what He expects you to contribute to His Kingdom.

13 January

"I tell you the truth, anyone who doesn't receive the Kingdom of God like a child will never enter it" (Mark 10:15, NLT).

Prayer Point

Children normally trust their parents and take their parent's word without asking questions. When God tells us something—like when he told Abram that He would be the father of many nations—He did not need to explain himself because He is able and nothing is impossible with Him.

As you dedicate your time to spend with God, pray that God teaches you to stay as humble as a child and to acknowledge your innocence in order to be receptive of His wisdom. Allow God to work through you that you may learn to respect people who share the Word of God and see beyond them to the source of their wisdom.

Pray for every nonbeliever that you have come across who believes in the power of self and not the power of God—that God can reveal

Himself in a mighty way through those people that they may be saved. Pray for yourself that you can start hearing and receiving from God in a mighty way.

14 January

"Jesus looked around and said to his disciples, 'How hard it is for the rich to enter the Kingdom of God!'" (Mark 10:23, NLT).

Prayer Point

Wealth should never become a substitute for God in our lives. It should remain the means by which God provides for us and others who may be less privileged than us as we are expected to share our wealth with them.

Pray that your relationship with God stays solid and that it remains consistent. Whether in lack or abundance, in need or rich, pray for His guidance that you may use His wealth in a manner that pleases Him, and to be a means by which you get others blessed through it.

Thank God for his provision in your life and pray for His help in prioritizing your life so that you may have everything being added unto you. Pray that you get spiritually rich so that other people can see God's Kingdom through you.

15 January

"For the Kingdom of God is not a matter of what we eat or drink, but of living a life of goodness and peace and joy in the Holy Spirit" (Romans 14:17, NLT).

I once met a man who testified that when he started out his business, he made sure that he got the office anointed, and he had Bible verse stickers almost everywhere in the office to show people and clients how much he believed in God. One thing that was not right was his heart with God. He confessed to using those stickers to cover up the fact that he felt guilty conducting business in a manner that did not please God completely.

God's Kingdom is not about displaying God's Word on the outside of a building or furniture. It has a lot to do with doing things with a heart that honours God and is fully in good standing with Him. God is more interested on the inside than the outside. You could eat and drink with cups, plates, and forks that have written Bible verses all around, but if your heart is full of things that are not pleasing to God, it will have no value.

The Kingdom of God goes beyond what we see physically and what our flesh is dependent upon. The kingdom of God is about being drawn to righteous living of goodness, peace, and joy that comes as a result of the transformation by the Holy Spirit in us.

The Kingdom of God is so important in our lives. When Jesus Christ taught His disciples how to pray the Lord's Prayer, He said, "Let thy Kingdom come." This is an indication that the Kingdom should be invited whenever we pray so that we can be in position to have the will of God manifest on earth, in our lives as it has taken place in heaven. Once the Kingdom is present in our lives, there will be peace, goodness, and joy in the Holy Spirit. This will be part of us—no matter how bad things may be in our lives. It is impossible to experience God's Kingdom without the presence of the Holy Spirit in our lives.

Prayer of the Day

Dear Lord, help me to live a life that will be pleasing to you—a life that will be full of peace and joy through the Holy Spirit. In the areas you know I lack, supplement my lack by the provision that will enable me to live a joyful life through the Holy Spirit. Restore all the days that I spent without peace, goodness, and joy—and multiply these by the power of the Holy Spirit, in Jesus's name. Amen.

16 January

"But he replied, 'I must preach the good news of the Kingdom of God in other towns, too, because that is why I was sent'" (Luke 4:43, NLT)

Prayer Point

The good news that Jesus came to preach is in the Bible. As His followers, you and I are expected to continue preaching the good news of God's Kingdom—love and grace. Share it with others so that they can be saved.

Pray that God can start using you from this season in a way that He wants to use you best as His vessel in His Kingdom. Read His Word so that you can continuously hear from Him and that He can reveal to you the things that He wants you to share with others about His Kingdom in Jesus's name.

Allow God to lead you to the appropriate method that you can use to preach His gospel—and to direct you to the target audience that He is preparing you to minister to. God has a specific audience for you; pray that He guides you on how you can reach out to that audience.

17 January

"Then Jesus turned to his disciples and said, 'God blesses you who are poor, for the Kingdom of God is yours'" (Luke 6:20, ISV).

Prayer Point

God is a father of both the rich and poor; when you feel poor, you may feel as if God has forsaken, but that is not true because God loves us the same whether we are rich or poor. The scripture says, "Blessed are the poor for the Kingdom of God is theirs."

You could be lacking different things in life, but know that God has not forsaken you. You are an heir of His Kingdom. Thank God for His love and grace.

Thank God for His Word for it is the truth; it does not contradict itself. Pray that He helps you to make His Kingdom a priority in your life—and that you can receive your blessings from Him.

18 January

"He replied, 'You are permitted to understand the secrets of the Kingdom of God. But I use parables to teach the others so that the Scriptures might be fulfilled: When they look, they won't really see. When they hear, they won't understand'" (Luke 8:10, NLT).

Prayer Point

God's Word as contained in the Bible has been inspired by God and brings life and wisdom to God's chosen people. God's Word is so powerful; it carries hidden knowledge that gets revealed to different people in different ways. Prayer is essential for understanding God's word.

As you devote the time to read God's word, pray that God can begin to reveal to you the things that have been hidden in His Word so that you can fully Hear and understand His word. Pray for understanding and revelation of His Word whenever you read it.

Pray that spiritual blindness and deafness be removed on every person that you share God's Word with. Pray that when you listen to God's Word, you may hear. Pray that when you look at God's Word, you may see.

19 January

"Then he sent them out to tell everyone about the Kingdom of God and to heal the sick" (Luke 9:2, NLT).

Prayer Point

Pray that God reveals to you His Kingdom in fullness that you may understand your role and be able to share it with people within your circle and be able to pray for the sick to be healed in Jesus's name.

As you continue to seek God's face and wisdom through prayer, continue trusting in Him for a responsibility that He wants you to start fulfilling if He has not already done so in your life. God is not a God of inactivity or laziness. He wants you to fulfill a special role in His Kingdom.

Thank Him for choosing you to be His servant that He can use you to tell everyone about God's Kingdom. Pray for the powerful experience of His Kingdom upon your life. Pray for the touching of people's lives through His Word.

20 January

"But Jesus told him, 'Let the spiritually dead bury their own dead! Your duty is to go and preach about the Kingdom of God'" (Luke 9:60, NLT).

Prayer Point

Preaching the Word of God is a duty that takes precedence over every other duty because of its significance. It requires spreading the good news and winning souls to Christ. How many times have you found yourself dedicating time to things that don't necessarily add value to the things of God?

No matter how busy your life is, always make an effort to share the good news of the Kingdom of Heaven. Rearrange your life in such a way that God's work is not last on your list of things you should do in a day.

Today, I invite you to pray that God leads you into doing the tasks that bear significance to His work.

21 January

"But Jesus told him, "Anyone who puts a hand to the plow and then looks back is not fit for the Kingdom of God'" (Luke 9:62, ESV).

Prayer Point

When you make a commitment to accept Jesus in your life and make Him your Savior, you are choosing to live a life that will honor Him through your works and through doing what He expects of you. In so doing, you will be working for God.

Working for God's Kingdom requires avoiding conflicting responsibilities. If you make a decision to plow forward in faith, you cannot keep looking back. Just as the Apostle Paul knew the importance of looking at the future, make it your priority not to dwell on things that happened in the past (Philippians 3:13-14).

Make it your prayer that, through Lord Jesus, you may continue serving Him. Never look back on the things that made you inactive and did not enable you to focus on your future or the present.

22 January

"For the Kingdom of God is not just a lot of talk; it is living by God's power" (1 Corinthians 4:20, NLT).

The emphasis on the Kingdom of God is on righteous living and living a life inspired by God through the Holy Spirit. Change the things of God that were not priorities into priorities. You have been listening to God's Word for a while and you have read the Word of God yourself. This time in your life must be a time when you act upon what the Word says and live by it.

You need to seek the Kingdom of God. Maintain a fellowship through constant connection and fellowship with God Almighty. Live a life from this day in accordance with the Kingdom standards and principles; get involved in executing tasks that are significant in God's kingdom (leading prayer groups, praying for the sick, or being an intercessor). To live a life that has the Kingdom's significance involves living a life of sacrifice. Your focus won't only be on you and your family. It will involve living a sacrifice where your life will be a gift and a benefit to people around you.

Scripture refers to the Kingdom of God as being able to live by the power of God; the Kingdom of God requires action. Something that has power often moves; it does not stay in one place. If you are only limiting yourself to what you can do in your own capacity, you can't do much by your own strength. However, if you allow the Holy Spirit to work through you (the power of God), then you will be doing what is required in the Kingdom of God. Once you start living for the Kingdom, your behaviour and the way you do things will be accelerated by the power of God. Aspire to be part of the Kingdom because that is where you belong. The enemy is a time thief; take stock of your time and make sure that God parts with a big share of it and that your efforts go into the things that bring glory to God.

Prayer of the Day

Dear God, make me seek your Kingdom in all areas of my life and strive to live under the influence and power of your Holy Spirit. I know that I'm nothing without you, but I'm somebody through your help, inspiration, and guidance.

Lead me in finding passion in the things pertinent to your Kingdom. Direct my steps to the things that will bring a smile on your face. Use my whole being for your glory. Use the words that come through my mouth as words that heal and not words that wound.

Help me, Lord Jesus, in the knowledge and understanding of you and make your light shine through me and attract many more people into your Kingdom in Jesus's name. Amen.

23 January

"'The time promised by God has come at last!' he announced. 'The Kingdom of God is near! Repent of your sins and believe the Good News!'"(Mark 1:15, NLT).

Prayer Point

There is no other time to long for righteousness than now. Different people over the centuries have made false predictions about the end of the world. Surely the actual date of the coming of Jesus Christ shouldn't even be a drive to living a righteous life because, as His followers, we should be living all our lives prepared for His return. Since it is inevitable that humankind will experience physical death, we need to stay prepared by our actions and our overall conduct.

In order to stay prepared to meet Lord Jesus, we need to continuously repent of our sins and live a Holy life. Lord Jesus is calling us to believe the good news of His gospel and to repent of our sins.

Make it a habit to repent of your sins regularly and pray that God may start using you in many different areas in your life for His glory. Temptations are everywhere; you need to stay alert and pray in order to protect your spirit and guard your heart.

24 January

"He replied, 'You are permitted to understand the secret of the Kingdom of God. But I use parables for everything I say to outsiders'" (Mark 4:11, NLT).

Prayer Point

God has given you the privilege to be one of those chosen people with the privilege to understand some of the secrets of His Kingdom. Use that privilege for your benefit, for the benefit of the Church, and to win more souls to Christ.

Set aside time on a daily basis to talk to God. By doing so, God will begin to reveal some of the things that you did not know. Make it your prayer that God reveals to you the secrets of His Kingdom through His Word and your ultimate role that He has designed for you to fulfill in His Kingdom.

With the permission that He has given to you to understand the secrets of the Kingdom, use the knowledge to share God's Word and to win souls to Christ. Use the knowledge with love—and not selfish ambition.

25 January

"Heal the sick, and tell them, 'The Kingdom of God is near you now'" (Luke 10:9, NLT).

Prayer Point

When Lord Jesus was on earth, He healed every person who believed and submitted to His authority. Some servants of God are also able to pray for others to get healed. It becomes important to tell someone who has received healing who previously did not know Jesus to be told that the Kingdom of God is near and to use that opportunity to tell people of God's grace and love.

Make it your prayer request to tell people in need of healing about the Healer who is Jesus when God starts using you in healing ministry. When people are inspired about the way you share the message of God, tell them about the Holy Spirit who has inspired you.

Invite the Holy Spirit of God to unleash your God-given abilities and talents. Renounce any form of bondage meant to deprive you of your God-given potential in the name of Jesus. Amen

26 January

"Repent of your sins and turn to God, for the Kingdom of Heaven is near," (Matthew 3:2, NLT).

Prayer Point

To repent refers to asking for forgiveness with the aim of maintaining a righteous life. When you turn to God, it's impossible that you can aim to please God whilst indulging in sin. You need to repent and then refocus and look at God who is a loving father and full of compassion.

Sin leads to the second death. You need to constantly scan your thoughts and actions and ask God to help you remove everything that is not of Him.

For as long as we live in the world that is full of sin, we have no option except to continuously repent and seek God's face and mercy. Pray that God grants you understanding on matters that seem complex—and enrich the persevering spirit within you that you may cross over to God's Kingdom in Jesus's name. Amen

27 January

"Jesus answered, 'Verily, verily, I say unto thee, Except a man be born of water and of the Spirit, he cannot enter into the kingdom of God'" (John 3:5, KJV).

Prayer Point

The Word of God is so clear and should be taken as it is for we will all be judged according to our works and our knowledge of the scriptures. Jesus says that unless that a man is born of water and of the spirit, he cannot enter the Kingdom of God.

Those requirements must be fulfilled by every believer accompanied by righteous living that will be as a result of the spiritual baptism. The water baptism cleanses our bodies from all the filthiness that our bodies have endured. Ezekiel 36:25 says, "Then I will sprinkle clean water on you, and you will be clean; I will cleanse you from all your filthiness and from all your idols."

Pray that God helps you receive and maintain this new baptism that you may enter the Kingdom of God.

28 January

"God is spirit, and his worshipers must worship in spirit and in truth" (John 4:24, NLT).

Prayer Point

God is a spiritual being and man has been created in His image. God requires us to have a fellowship with Him, to spend time with Him, and to tell Him of His goodness and mercies in our lives. When we draw near to God and we start worshipping Him, we must worship Him in Spirit and in truth for He is near to all who call on him in truth (Psalm 145:18).

God knows our thoughts and the desires of our hearts. We cannot fake our love for Him because He knows our hearts in full. He wants us to worship Him in spirit and in truth; our actions should conform to what we say we have set our minds to concerning our relationship with Him.

Pray that God shows you how you should worship Him in a manner that will be pleasing to Him. Get in the habit of pleasing God by worshipping Him in spirit and in truth.

29 January

"Seek the Lord and his strength, seek his face continually" (1 Chronicles 16:11, ESV).

Prayer Point

When you seek something, you have gone beyond looking for something and are literally searching for something. When you search for something, you will need to put in extra effort and go to different places to find whatever that you are looking for.

When you are seeking the Lord, seek the Lord in prayer through His Word. You may tune into television channels or radio stations that preach the Word of God to hear what God is saying to you concerning your current situation.

In my Christian walk, I came to conclude that God is everywhere—but not in everything. You have to continually seek Him in those right places in order to find Him. You cannot expect to hear from God when you are occupying your mind with the things of this world. If you allow your flesh to submit and get your spiritual being elevated through prayer and reading His Word, you will be seeking God and His strength. Aim to seek God continuously.

30 January

"Being confident of this very thing, that he which hath begun a good work in you will perform it until the day of Jesus Christ" (Philippians 1:6, KJV).

Prayer Point

When you give your life to Christ and say, "Lord, here I am with all my weaknesses and my sins. Please cleanse me with your blood as I receive you as my Lord and personal saviour," good work has ultimately begun in you.

Be confident that the good work through Jesus has begun in you from the day that you became saved from your sins. You could be someone who is not proud of who you are and the kind of life that you led before you received Christ. Maybe you were involved in drug dealing or were a sex addict or committed abortions. God is telling you to leave the past behind and look at the bright future ahead of you. He has started good work in you that He will perform until the day of Jesus Christ.

Ask the Holy Spirit of God to give you the wisdom to work in confidence. Allow the Holy Spirit to unveil the hidden treasures that God has deposited in you for His glory. Refuse to be held back by your weaknesses from the past. Continue believing in God's favour upon your life.

31 January

"Lead me in thy truth, and teach me: for thou art the God of my salvation; on thee do I wait all the day" (Psalms 25:5, ESV).

Prayer Point

God is a God of truth; anything that contradicts the truth comes from the evil one. When you make a prayer request about something for which you need a revelation, ask God to lead you into the whole truth concerning the matter.

Sometimes it only takes knowing the truth about a situation for one to seriously pray the right prayer. It is possible to spend our entire lives believing the enemy's lie—it would make us believe that it's okay to be sick because sickness runs in the family. When God leads you into His truth, you will rebuke the curse of those diseases in your family because you would know that we have been healed by the stripes of Jesus.

Wait upon the Lord and His truth and accept and live by it. You are set free by God's truth. The blood of Jesus that flows through you has washed down all the curses and you are ready for more blessings.

Chapter 2

Love at All Times:
Remembering That God Is Love

1 February

"Create in me a pure heart, O God, and renew a steadfast spirit within me" (Psalm 51:10, NIV).

A pure heart holds no bitterness, anger, or hatred—only love. A pure heart is what the psalmist longed for after realizing that his thoughts and ways of living were not in line with God's heart because David had just committed adultery with Bathsheba. He felt the need to have God create a pure heart and renew a spirit within him.

In life, we may come across situations that can alter the good character that we initially had. These situations can present themselves in different ways; if we are not strong enough, the spirit inside of us can get corrupted and our minds can start to think of things that are not pure. Since God looks at the heart, if it is not in pure, then actions are not pure and we could even start saying things that are not pure. It is important to remember that a man is not made unclean because of what goes inside; he is made unclean because of the things that come out of his mouth(Mark 7:15).

Things that pollute the heart are things such as adultery, hatred, envy, jealousy, and many other things that do not demonstrate the fruits of the Spirit.

The things that pollute the heart can hinder one from praying and living a life that pleases God. God looks at the heart of a person; He is pleased when the heart is pure. The psalmist longed for a pure heart—and that is what we all need in order to love.

If someone has wronged you in the past few days and you are finding it hard to let go, allow God to create a pure heart in you and renew that Spirit within you. It is impossible for love and hate to coexist in one heart; where there is bitterness, true love cannot be found.

Prayer of the Day

Dear Father, remove everything that is not pure in me and replace it with pure and loving thoughts. Renew my mind, spirit, and soul so that I can please you. In Jesus's name, help me to change some of my thoughts and actions that are not pleasing in your sight. Replace them with the love that comes from you. In Jesus's name. Amen.

2 February

"Dear friends, let us love one another, for love comes from God. Everyone who loves has been born of God and knows God. Whoever does not love does not know God, because God is love" (1 John 4:7-8 NIV).

Prayer Point

When your life is under the influence of God through the Holy Spirit, you will find it easy to love. Love describes who God truly is; anyone who is a believer should be able to love. Anyone who has been born of God should love.

Ask God to ignite your spirit with love, love for your family, friends, in-laws and even your enemies. Hate is not of God; love is from God because God is love.

Pray for the love of God to spread in everything you do so that you can do it fully in accordance with the way that God expects of you.

3 February

"A new commandment I give to you, that you love one another: just as I have loved you, you also are to love one another. By this all people will know that you are my disciples, if you have love for one another" (John 13:34-35, NIV).

Prayer Point

In addition to the commandments that were given to Moses by God, Jesus Christ has added a new commandment: love one another as He has loved us. Jesus is more interested in how we share the love that we have received from Him with other people.

Anything that opposes the love of God through Christ Jesus is not of God. Jesus has left us with this new commandment. As His followers, we can differentiate ourselves as Christians by how we love one another.

Pray that God helps you to love others as Jesus has loved you. Ask God to lead you into questioning your motive every time you do something that is not out of love so that you can stop doing it and instead act out of love.

4 February

"This is my commandment, that you love one another as I have loved you. Greater love has no one than this: that someone lays down his life for his friends. You are my friends if you do what I command you" (John 15:12-14, ESV).

Prayer Point

Jesus demonstrated His love for us by giving up His very own life in order for you and me to be saved. He had committed no sin, but He made the decision to give up His life for us so that we can be saved for as long as we believe in Him. He had far greater love for us because not even your brother, sister, or parents can be willing to give up their lives to save you should situations demand. People often run to save their own lives when things get bad; however, Jesus was interested in saving you by paying the price for you.

We are Jesus's friend if we do what He commands us to do. Jesus wants us to be likeminded with Him through our actions and the things that we speak. If the things we speak are inspired by love, we can surely see Christ living in us and working through us.

Pray that God leads you into loving other people—just as Christ loved you. Even in circumstances where you feel that no one deserves your love, love them in the manner that God loves you unconditionally.

5 February

"And this is his commandment: that we believe in the name of His Son Jesus Christ and love one another just as He has commanded us. Whoever keeps His commandments abides in Him, and He in them. And by this we know that he abides in us, by the Spirit whom he has given us (1 John 3:23-24, NLT).

Prayer Point

As a child, your parents have expectations from you that include living a life full of respect and obedience to the good things that they teach you. When you are a very good child, your parents become proud of you. A disobedient child brings disappointment to the parents. The same is true when we become disobedient to God's commandments. When we live in accordance with God's expectation—living in love and showing love to others—we can be confident that we are abiding in Jesus.

When you abide in Jesus, you fully accept His fullness to take over your being. Make it your prayer request that you focus on living in God's fullness.

Allow the Word of God to sink in your spirit. You will bear fruit of love and abide in Christ Jesus through continuous sharing of his love with other people.

6 February

"First of all, then, I urge that supplications, prayers, intercessions, and thanksgivings be made for all people, for kings and all who are in high positions, that we may lead a peaceful and quiet life, godly and dignified in every way" (1 Timothy 2:1-2, ESV).

Prayer Point

The love of God will make you pray an unselfish prayer for other people on earth who may not even know that you have prayed for them. You would have prayed for them in any event because you would have sensed their need for a prayer. The love of God will not make you think of yourself as an important person. It will make you consider the needs of others and stand in the gap for them during prayer and when you make special intercessions.

Allow the Holy Spirit in your life to direct your heart to identify the needs of others and the needs of your church and your country. God's love can take full control so that peace, joy, and righteousness can prevail for love never fails (1 Corinthians 13:8).

Thank God for emphasising the importance of love through his Word through Christ Jesus. Pray for different people in different positions that God meet their needs.

7 February

"There is no fear in love, but perfect love casts out fear. For fear has to do with punishment, and whoever fears has not been perfected in love. We love because He first loved us" (1 John 4:18-19, NIV).

Prayer Point

When Lord Jesus was faced with death on the cross and having to imagine what He would go through as the hour drew near, one important thing that kept Him going was to see us saved by His love. The love He had for us was so strong that it overcame any trace of fear He could have had.

We are expected to love in a way that would eliminate all the fear and doubt in our hearts because perfect love casts out fear. If you have been hurt numerous times in your life, you may be afraid to love because you are worried that what happened to you in the past could happen again. Living in fear is another form of bondage because we have more than we need through the love of God.

Pray that the fear in your heart be replaced by the genuine love that comes from our Lord and Saviour Jesus Christ. Pray that God helps you to extend your love so that you can live in faith through Him.

8 February

"'Look,'" said Naomi, 'your sister-in-law is going back to her people and her gods. Go back with her.' But Ruth replied, 'Don't urge me to leave you or to turn back from you. Where you go, I will go, and where you stay, I will stay. Your people will be my people and your God my God. Where you die, I will die, and there I will be buried. May the Lord deal with me, be it ever so severely, if anything but death separates you and me.' When Naomi realized that Ruth was determined to go with her, she stopped urging her." (Ruth 1:15-18, NIV).

The Book of Ruth is very short book that illustrates the love that Naomi and Ruth had for each other. It is the rare kind of love that one would not expect to find between mother and daughter-in-law. This devotional is meant to show that when you love someone, it should not be based on conditions or circumstances. Love must continue even if the events that led you to meet have significantly changed like it was for Naomi and Ruth.

I know of a sad story about a married couple who had a car accident. The husband, a doctor, was badly injured and it became impossible to practice as a doctor. He had to stay at home; as a result, the wife divorced him because he was no longer the doctor that she had married. This story shows that the love this woman had was dependant on everything remaining the same. Since the car accident altered everything, she had no love for the husband anymore.

Ruth demonstrated a different kind of love where—despite the death of her husband—she had a very loving character. She boldly committed to Naomi by saying that she was not turning back—no matter what. This scripture shows us that love is a genuine responsibility. You need to give love to people—your family, friends, and everyone you come across. In this verse, God is illustrating love as a sacrifice because Ruth made a choice to remain with Naomi because she loved her so much. It could be that Naomi had shown Ruth so much love even before her son died that when Ruth thinks of that love, she finds it difficult to let go.

This scripture is so profound in that the love portrayed here emphasizes denying oneself for the benefit of the other. That is what our Lord Jesus Christ did for us at the cross; He sacrificed His life for us out of love. Let us be reminded today that telling someone that you love them is not enough on its own. Taking a step of love and making a sacrifice when needed is an act of love.

Prayer of the Day

Dear Heavenly Father, I want to thank you for showing me how much you love me through your son, Jesus Christ. I ask you to give me the strength to love my family, friends, and everybody through the love that has no limits. I'm asking all these in the wonderful name of my Lord and Saviour, Jesus Christ of Nazareth. Amen

9 February

"Love is patient and kind; love does not envy or boast; it is not arrogant or rude. It does not insist on its own way; it is not irritable or resentful; it does not rejoice at wrongdoing, but rejoices with the truth. Love bears all things, believes all things, hopes all things, endures all things" (1 Corinthians 13:4-7, ESV).

Prayer Point

Sometimes we get caught up in situations where we are not sure if we are acting out of love or hate. The scripture here is clear as to how love can be described. Being impatient with others and easily give up on them is not an act of love. According to the scripture, love is patient and patience goes with kindness.

When your heart gets filled with love, you don't get irritated or live a life full of bitterness or resentment. You will know that you have a loving spirit within you when you start to persevere in all things.

Ask God to help you live a life that is love-driven. Pray that the Holy Spirit helps you refrain from any behaviour that is not an act of love. Let go of any act of envy, boastful attitude, or any behaviour that is not Christ-like. Allow love to fill your heart so that you can be more patient and rejoice at the truth.

10 February

"If I speak in the tongues of men and of angels, but have not love, I am a noisy gong or a clanging cymbal. And if I have prophetic powers, and understand all mysteries and all knowledge, and if I have all faith, so as to remove mountains, but have not love, I am nothing. If I give away all I have, and if I deliver up my body to be burned, but have not love, I gain nothing" (1 Corinthians 13:1-3, NIV).

Prayer Point

God has blessed many people on earth with different gifts or abilities. Some people are good at art, some are strategists, and some are good at looking after nature and the interests of animals. In the church, there are numerous gifts that people possess. Some are able to teach God's Word and others have the gift to prophesy, but all these gifts are there for us to be able to serve according to the way God expects us to serve.

It is common for people to serve in the house of the Lord by singing or teaching the Word without having their hearts open to love. The scripture above reminds us that no gift or ability is greater than love itself. The love of God and the love for one another bring glory to God.

If God has blessed you with the gift to prophesy, but you are full of envy or jealousy, you may choose to withhold the Word of edification to a fellow Christian. However, if you have God's love in your heart, you will use God's gift in a way that is kind and true. Identify areas in your life where God has blessed you and let the Holy Spirit guide you into using those gifts with love. This may require you to pray for people you dislike or to prophesy for people that you would normally not. Ask God to allow you to use your gifts in love for the glory of His Kingdom.

11 February

"And give no opportunity to the devil" (Ephesians 4:27, ESV).

Prayer Point

A heart that is not full of love is prone to giving the devil opportunities to destroy you and others. It would be very difficult to celebrate the successes of other people without love in your heart.

Pray that God occupies your whole heart through His spirit that will teach you how to love. Pray that the gaps that are open in your life due to past hurts or disappointments, which may make it difficult for you to love, be removed in Jesus's name.

Ask the Holy Spirit to constantly remind you of God's loving mercies and kindness. When you are faced with an opportunity to show love and kindness, aim to do as He expects you to. Pray that your life be love-proofed so that the devil does not get an opportunity to influence your life.

12 February

"Get rid of all bitterness, rage and anger, brawling and slander, along with every form of malice" (Ephesians 4:31, NIV).

Prayer Point

Moments that make it possible to love God wholeheartedly and to love others come as soon as we let go of everything that is not godly. Things such as bitterness and anger that are inside of us cause spiritual toxicity.

Love cannot coexist with all the things that are holding us back. Everything that causes us pain has happened in the past, but love is full of hope because it is based on trust and faith in God. Love looks forward.

Pray that God delivers you from all the things of the past and gives you fresh hope for the future through His love through Christ Jesus.

13 February

"Rejoice in the Lord always; again I will say, rejoice. Let your reasonableness be known to everyone. The Lord is at hand; do not be anxious about anything, but in everything by prayer and supplication with thanksgiving let your requests be made known to God" (Philippians 4:4-6, NIV).

Prayer Point

A heart that is filled with God's love, peace, and contentment will always be a heart that is full of praise; it will be a joyous heart. Rejoice in the Lord and become filled with understanding. Have absolute faith in God knowing that He has you in His hand.

Whatever your needs are today, thank God for the breath that you are still taking and continue to grow and believe in His love. God is in control—even if you don't feel Him—but His love never ends. Don't give up in being joyous; trust His love for you.

Pray that no circumstance or challenge consumes your entire love reservoir; God's love has no end or limits. Pray for more love to abound in your life so that others may be drawn to love through you.

14 February

"And let us consider how to stir up one another to love and good works, not neglecting to meet together, as is the habit of some, but encouraging one another, and all the more as you see the Day drawing near" (Hebrews 10:24-25, ESV).

Prayer Point

As a child of God, God wants to use you to demonstrate His love for others through you. When God has put you in a position of leadership, such as being a prayer group leader, He trusts you to attract more people to His prayer group by having you show love, pray for others, and encourage others who may be discouraged. God does not expect us as His children to stir up hatred through gossip because that kills the church. God expects us to stir each other to love and good works.

Pray that your involvement in things of God demonstrates the love that will draw other people to Christ. Pray that your actions and words attract other people to Christ so that they may stay attracted to the things of God.

The Word of God today is meant for your encouragement. After you have been encouraged, you may also encourage others. Pray that the love of God in you will bear fruit so that you may be able to meet and encourage other people in a manner that will show God's love.

15 February

"We love because he first loved us. If anyone says, 'I love God,' and hates his brother, he is a liar; for he who does not love his brother whom he has seen cannot love God whom he has not seen. And this commandment we have from him: whoever loves God must also love his brother" (1 John 4:19-21, ESV).

Quite often it is easier to receive love than to show or give love. To love someone whom you have nothing to gain from can even be more difficult; it feels good to love people that we benefit from doing so. As children of God, we are commanded to love because love defines our entire relationship with our Lord and Saviour, Jesus Christ. If God did not love us, there would be no salvation because Jesus would not have died in order for our sins to be forgiven. God has demonstrated his love for us by allowing His Son Jesus Christ to die so that anyone who believes in Him should not perish but have eternal life. God expects us to exercise our love by loving anyone—be it our family, friends, or people that we feel do not deserve to be loved by us. We are also expected to love our enemies and pray for those who persecute us (Matthew 5:44).

By loving everyone—even the people we deem unlovable—we are fulfilling the commandment of love. The major cause of conflict in the world today is due to a lack of love. People kill because of lack of love. People steal because of lack of love. People can't give good gifts to others because they lack love for them. People can't forgive because of pride and lack of love. However, when love is present, anything good becomes possible. God works best where there is love.

From today, when someone wrongs you, see it as an opportunity to love. God always knows our hearts and the most suitable way to correct people who wrong us. Our responsibility is to show love and not judge.

Prayer of the Day

Dear Lord, replace any hatred I have for my brothers, parents, in-laws, and sisters with the true love that comes from you. Help me forgive everyone who has wronged me in the past so that I can open my heart to the complete and genuine love that you want me to show. Thank you, Lord, for loving me first before I even knew myself. Be my guide dear, Lord, in Jesus's name. Amen.

16 February

"Let love be genuine. Abhor what is evil; hold fast to what is good. Love one another with brotherly affection. Outdo one another in showing honour" (Romans 12:9-10, ESV).

Prayer Point

You can be certain that shoes made of genuine leather will last longer than shoes made of artificial leather. This scripture instructs us to let love be genuine so that it can last and can take us to places we would otherwise not get to if it were not genuine. When love is genuine— even if it gets tested—it will never fail.

My prayer for you today is that you can cling to what is good and hate what is evil. God expects you to live a life of goodness that is inspired by love and kindness. Scripture says that love does not rejoice with evil but with the truth (1 Corinthians 13:6).

Pray and ask God to reveal to you the areas that you need to show more love and respect. Allow the Holy Spirit to teach you to love genuinely in areas where you have been pretending or battling to show true love.

17 February

"Let all that you do be done in love" (1 Corinthians 16:14, ESV).

Prayer Point

I have come across many people in my life who God has blessed with good jobs. Surprisingly, many of them do not conform to love; some work just to fulfil while some would make up any excuse not to pitch for work. If all mankind did everything in love, the world would be a better place to live.

Doing all that we do in love can only happen when we condition our minds and practice doing every task in love. Some patients would not die unnecessarily if their caretakers in hospital did all they could out of love and not out of duty.

Allow the Holy Spirit to help you serve and work in love. Let all your actions be driven by love. Let it be your prayer to God that He enables you to love one another sincerely (Romans 12:9). Don't dwell too much on the mistakes of other people; look at the good they do.

18 February

"Husbands, love your wives, as Christ loved the church and gave himself up for her" (Ephesians 5:25, NIV).

Prayer Point

God has expectations for all of us—husbands, wives, and children. When we face judgment, God will judge us in accordance with how we lived to fulfil His commands for our roles. This verse states that husbands must love their wives as Jesus Christ loved the church. The Word of God is very clear because it does not say that husbands should criticize or dishonour their wives. It says that they should love their wives.

Seek the guidance of God to love accordingly in all the relationships in your life—and in the measure expected of you by God. Love your children the way God expects you to love them—and do the same with your parents or spouse.

Pray that God opens up your heart and mind to love your wife, husband, and children as God expects of you so that you may grow in obedience to God.

19 February

"You shall treat the stranger who sojourns with you as the native among you, and you shall love him as yourself, for you were strangers in the land of Egypt: I am the Lord your God" (Leviticus 19:34, ESV).

Prayer Point

We are bound to meet and interact with people who are not born-again Christians. God does not expect us to love only the people who have been saved through Christ Jesus. People who are strangers in the Kingdom of God may come our way to ask for help.

We were once strangers in Christ Jesus because of sin, but He redeemed us of our sins and made us new creatures. With the same love that we received from Christ, God expects us to love other strangers in Christ Jesus as God has loved us.

Pray that your heart may be open to people who may be strangers in Christ. God wants to show Himself through you to strangers with the love and kindness that He expects you to show to others. You should love a stranger in Christ Jesus as yourself. Accept all the strangers in your life and love them. You were a stranger to Christ before you received Him as your Saviour; every person deserves to be loved.

20 February

"You have heard that it was said, 'You shall love your neighbour and hate your enemy.' But I say to you, 'Love your enemies and pray for those who persecute you'" (Matthew 5:43-44, ESV).

Prayer Point

When Jesus Christ died for our sins on Calvary, He was not doing it to take away some of our sins or problems. He did it to take away all the problems and pain. He is ultimately responsible for blessing those who love us and handle all the people who hate us.

Jesus knows the cause of any enmity; if we could avenge people for the hate they show us, there would be much chaos in the world. Christ will deal with whoever wrongs us because He sees everything—even what is hidden in the darkness.

Our responsibility as Christians is not to hate back, but to love. When we love, we get to defeat the enemy and his tricks. If we return evil with evil, we lose the fight to the devil for he is in favour of agony. I urge you to pray for those who persecute you; God will take care of the rest.

21 February

Blessed are you when others revile you and persecute you and utter all kinds of evil against you falsely on My account. Rejoice and be glad for your reward is great in heaven (Matthew 5:11-12, ESV).

Prayer Point

There are certain moments where the goodness in your heart cannot freely manifest because of the circumstances around you. Sometimes people can make wrong assumptions about the person that you are—or judge the person that God has created you to be. As a result, it could be difficult to show love in the midst of all the allegations. It could be that you got married to a family of unbelievers and you constantly get mocked by some of your family members for being a Christian.

The Word of God is encouraging us to focus on Jesus because blessed is anyone who is falsely accused for Jesus's Christ sake. Even though you don't see it now, your reward is great in heaven.

Pray that God gives you the strength to love despite being falsely accused by different people. Pray that you continue pressing toward the mark of the high calling in Christ Jesus (Philippians 3:14). As the accusations increase, increase your love for your enemies in Jesus's name.

22 February

"Most important of all, continue to show deep love for each other, for love covers a multitude of sins" (1 Peter 4:8, NLT).

During high school, I found it very hard to forgive. When someone wronged me, I would not easily get it off my mind. Whenever I met that person, I would be overwhelmed with anger and sadness. Another thing that I used to do was to keep an accurate record of all the wrongs that a person had done. When they asked for forgiveness, I would tell them that it was not the first time they were doing this to me and I would continue being angry. I would refuse to accept that person as a friend for a very long time.

When I got married, I realised that this is the institution where this verse has to apply because, as husband and wife, you constantly upset each other. The love you have for each other overcomes all the shortcomings in your marriage.

Love is such a powerful force because love does not keep a record of wrongs; it covers a multitude of sins. When something is covered, it means you don't intend to see what has been covered—not even the form of that mistake. When genuine love is present, multitudes of sins are covered so that they are never retrieved as a point of reference.

It is only when love is deep within you—that even when the most precious thing in your life has been taken away—that you are able to forgive and remember the sin no more.

Prayer of the Day

Dear Lord, grant me the ability to correct all the wrongs in my life with love. Let me always remember the sacrifices you made on the cross through your Son, Jesus Christ, who was sinless but had to die to wipe away all our sins. Lord, I want to always remember and respect the fact that in order to remove darkness, the light must shine upon it. Let my light of love shine upon all the people I used to hate. In Jesus's name. Amen.

23 February

"For you were called to freedom, brothers. Only do not use your freedom as an opportunity for the flesh, but through love serve one another. For the whole law is fulfilled in one word: 'You shall love your neighbour as yourself'" (Galatians 5:13-14, ESV).

Prayer Point

In our society, we see very few role models when it comes to showing love to others. Often, it is a norm in certain countries to have certain classes of people prefer to be served than to serve others.

When an opportunity presents itself to make donations of clothes to impoverished communities, some people see it as an opportunity to buy new clothes that they would want to wear themselves and give those away, but others just think of cleaning their house of all unwanted and torn clothes that they would not want to wear and give those items away.

God expects us to love our neighbours as we would like others to love us by giving them the gifts that we would like to receive or giving them the food that we would like to eat. Pray that God may help you to serve in love and to love in a manner you would like to be loved.

24 February

"Owe no one anything, except to love each other, for the one who loves another has fulfilled the law" (Romans 13:8, ESV)

Prayer Point

There are things we need God to help us guard our hearts against so that they do not hinder us to love. Jealousy can prevent us from loving each other. Competition among families and sibling rivalry can rob us of opportunities to genuinely love each other.

The Word of God reminds us that we must not owe anyone anything except loving each other because that is how we fulfil the law.

Pray for God to reveal the people who you need to show more love and kindness to in your life. Give them any gift you might have. Pray for them or sacrifice some of the belongings or time that you may have to spend with them.

25 February

"By this it is evident who the children of God are, and who are the children of the devil: whoever does not practice righteousness is not of God, nor is the one who does not love his brother. For this is the message that you have heard from the beginning, that we should love one another" (1 John 3:10–11, ESV).

Prayer Point

God wants us to live a life that is full of righteousness and goodness—and does not contradict itself. Someone who loves and says so will testify if they are acting out of love or if they are deceptive.

Today presents an opportunity to determine whether your ways are taking you to God or to the evil one. Look at whether your life is full of righteousness and love for your brothers.

Pray that your life is filled with goodness and that you pursue righteousness in every aspect of your life. God does not get deceived by us because He looks at what is inside our hearts. He can tell if our love for others is genuine or fake. Do the things that Christ would do and stay away from the ways of the evil one.

26 February

"For God loved the world so much that he gave his one and only Son, so that everyone who believes in him will not perish but have eternal life" (John 3:16, NIV).

Prayer Point

God realised that because the world was blind because of sin. Everyone was living in darkness and born into sin. He saw the need to give us a Saviour. God is full of mercy; He did not want us to perish. He sent His only Son to come and die for our sins so that whoever believes in Jesus would not die but have everlasting life.

As a believer in Christ Jesus, have you ever wondered what the sacrifice that Jesus made for you on the cross meant to you? I would like you to thank God for the blood of Jesus.

Thank God for the most precious gift of His love through Jesus Christ our redeemer who paid the price for you and me to obtain the benefit of eternal life. Treasure the gift of love and extend or share it with others.

27 February

"That is what the Scriptures mean when they say, 'No eye has seen, no ear has heard, and no mind has imagined what God has prepared for those who love him'" (1 Corinthians 2:9, NLT).

Prayer Point

To love God is to live all your life for Him in accordance with His commands for you. God wants you to first demonstrate the concept of love by acting out of love and showing love and kindness to your brothers, sisters, and others.

God has made preparations for people who have loved Him. Only God has seen these things.

Thank God for revealing how you can love Him—by loving your brothers and neighbours in the manner that you would like to be loved. We were all created by God; when we love each other, we are fulfilling the law.

28 February

"Three things will last forever—faith, hope, and love—and the greatest of these is love" (1 Corinthians 13:13, NLT).

Prayer Point

All things on earth someday shall pass away. The relationships that we have with other people, material possessions, and other things will pass away. We experience the reality of this when we lose people that we were very close to.

The Word of God assures us that there are three things that will last forever: faith in God, hope in God, and love. These are heavenly attributes. When you are in heaven, you will continue having faith in God and loving God.

Allow the Holy Spirit to get your mind accustomed to doing things out of love and looking for an opportunity to love. Love is the greatest commandment and will remain after everything.

29 February

"What sorrow awaits you, Pharisees! For you are careful to tithe even the tiniest income from your herb gardens, but you ignore justice and the love of God. You should tithe, yes, but do not neglect the more important things" (Luke 11:42, NLT).

Prayer Point

As part of our Christian responsibilities, we ought to go to church and pay offerings and tithes. That does not mean that we can overlook certain important things of God—showing love to others, praying for peace, and seeking justice—because we pay what is due.

The Pharisees knew their responsibilities and chose where they could be fully obedient. They chose to be obedient on things that were measurable on their sight and quantifiable and neglected things that mattered even though we cannot precisely quantify the amount of justice or the love for God.

You ought to live a balanced Christian life that takes into account your responsibilities in the house of the Lord: offering and tithing, loving the Lord, and seeking justice in our communities, families, and the world.

Chapter 3

Forgive In All Situations, So That You Can Also Be Forgiven

1 March

"If we confess our sins, He is faithful and just to forgive us our sins and to cleanse us from all unrighteousness" (1 John 1:9, ESV).

God saw the need to have his son nailed on the cross because all mankind had sinned and we fell short of God's glory. The blood of Jesus was the only solution that could cleanse and purify us of our unrighteousness. When you accept Jesus as your Lord and Saviour, you become a new creature. Old things pass away and you begin to live a new life. When God forgives your sins, He does not remember your old sins. He basically gives you a clean sheet to start writing your new life on. Even if you used to be a murderer, when God has forgiven you, He does not remind you of your past. He knows that sad memories would steal your joy of the present. God gives you a new life with no sad memories through His Son Jesus. Jesus forgave even the people who crucified Him. He asked God to forgive those people who were going to kill Him. Luke 23:34 reveals Jesus as someone who is merciful and full of love.

The Lord is faithful; He has paid the price for us so that our sins can be forgiven and our unrighteousness can be cleansed.

You could be reading this devotional today knowing deep down that you have done terrible things that have made you live in bondage for a very long time. This is a special call to you to ask God to forgive you of those sins because there is no sin that God cannot forgive. Allow

Jesus to cleanse you of all your righteousness in order to live a free, spirit-filled life.

Prayer of the Day

Dear God, thank you for your faithfulness, kindness, generosity, and all the things that you have blessed me with. Thank you for showing your love through the sacrifice you made through your son, Jesus. Lead me to live a life full of righteousness and mercy. Help me to live a life which will be exemplary to other people around me in Jesus's name. Amen.

2 March

"But there is forgiveness with thee, that thou mayest be feared" (Psalm 130:4, KJV).

Prayer Point

The enemy often whispers lies into our thoughts that a sin will not be forgiven. You are likely to find yourself living in guilt and being so limited in your thoughts that you cannot progress in life because of this guilt. God will always forgive your sins if you ask Him so that He can receive glory and be feared.

Allow God to release you from your doubt and feelings of low self-esteem because of mistakes you have committed. Look to God for assurance and forgiveness; He is interested in loving you and seeing you grow in the knowledge of Him.

There could be times when you have sinned against others: you could have said something hurtful to others, lied to someone, or disappointed your children, spouse, or parents. Ask God to forgive you for all these sins; there is forgiveness of sins through Jesus Christ and you will be set free from guilt.

3 March

"To the Lord our God belong mercies and forgivenesses, though we have rebelled against him" (Daniel 9:9, KJV).

Prayer Point

I have seen God being such a merciful father in countless circumstances. God's mercies carry us through difficult situations. Mercy and forgiveness belong to God, but we have to ask for mercy and forgiveness from Him.

Sometimes other people can make you feel that you depend on their mercies and their forgiveness to carry on with life. However, if God has seen your heart and your humble attitude when you sought forgiveness, He is able to forgive you for all your sins. People can withhold their forgiveness, but God does not.

Pray for the mercies of God to see you through within your family, work, as you travel to different places, as you grow in faith and understanding.

4 March

"And forgive us our debts, as we forgive our debtors" (Matthew 6:12, ESV).

Prayer Point

As humans, we are not perfect. We are likely to upset each other now and then and to ask for forgiveness from each other. Since no one on earth is perfect, we are bound to wrong one another in different ways.

When we stand in prayer at any time, we need to make sure that we forgive anyone who has wronged us with an understanding that we are also not perfect—and we also need continuous forgiveness from God.

Just as you also wrong others and beg for their forgiveness, you must forgive others before you pray so that when you seek forgiveness from God, He may grant you considering that you do the same. Pray that God helps you to value the benefits of being able to forgive others.

5 March

"For if ye forgive men their trespasses, your heavenly Father will also forgive you" (Matthew 6:14, KJV).

Prayer Point

The word "if" sets out a condition to the issue around forgiveness on this verse because it basically says that in order for you to be forgiven you have a responsibility to forgive everyone who has wronged you.

Guard your heart against self-righteousness where you may think that you are a perfect person who offends no one. Even if you have not offended anyone today, you don't know what you can do that may offend others tomorrow. A burst water pipe that spills water on your neighbour's yard and damages their property may require you to seek forgiveness.

Allow the Holy Spirit to help you release past hurts, failures, and grudges that arose out of disappointments from others. Pray that God helps you to see every person the way that He sees them so that it can be easy for you to forgive them.

6 March

"But if ye forgive not men their trespasses, neither will your Father forgive your trespasses" (Matthew 6:15, KJV).

Prayer Point

To forgive someone can be such a difficult challenge when you know that someone intentionally wronged you or they are not offending you for the first time. The Word of God reminds us that if we withhold forgiveness, God won't set us free.

Pray for your mind to be free of resentment. As you seek to be forgiven by God, acknowledge your mistakes and imperfections. Humble yourself and be prepared to forgive everyone who has wronged you.

Do not allow disappointments to harden your heart to a point where you find it difficult to forgive. Resentment does not change the fact; forgiveness changes your world and improves you relationship with God.

7 March

"While they were stoning him, Stephen prayed, 'Lord Jesus, receive my spirit.' Then he fell on his knees and cried out, 'Lord, do not hold this sin against them.' When he had said this, he fell asleep (Acts 7:59-60, NIV).

Prayer Point

Many of us have such a difficulty with forgiving those who wrong us, but we are still alive unlike Stephen who saw that there was no chance of survival. Some people are so good at stating the number of years that they have not talked to a particular person because that person wronged them. If we fail to forgive while we are still alive, how about if we were in the same situation as Stephen where we would know that we are being stoned with the intention of being killed?

Beloved, I urge you to ask God to reveal to you the importance of forgiveness and ask you to have a heart like Stephen's. Forgive those who persecute you; if you forgive, God will give you the same mercy that you have given others.

Pray that God builds into your spirit a forgiving attitude so that you can forgive with understanding of the power that comes with it.

8 March

"If your enemy is hungry, feed him; if he is thirsty, give him something to drink. In doing this, you will heap burning coals on his head. Do not be overcome by evil but overcome evil with good (Romans 12:20-21, NIV).

In life, we meet people who impact our lives in different ways. Some people walked in our lives for such a short time, but they added so much value to our lives. Some were in our lives for a short while, but they caused us pain that can cause emotional paralysis. As we get this emotional pain constantly rubbed against our hearts, it becomes human nature to feel that burning sensation of paying revenge that would be contrary to what God expects us to do.

God expects us to feed our enemies to counteract the pain our enemies cause us. He basically wants us not just to forgive those who wrong us; He wants us to act in love toward those who hurt us. If we had to compete by returning evil for evil, then we would no longer be any good to God's Kingdom. We would be doing what the enemy wants—never-ending conflict and pain.

Forgiveness is the same as saying "God, I hand over this person who wronged me to you so that you can deal with him/her in the manner you deem appropriate." Sometimes people wrong us—not because they always plan to but because the enemy got to manipulate them for a moment and used them to offend us. If we always judge things by our emotions and what we see physically, our judgment will be partial because we may not have the full revelation of what is happening in the spiritual realm. This can be confirmed by the scripture found in Ephesians 6:12: "For our struggle is not against flesh and blood, but against the authorities, against the authorities, against the powers of this dark world and against the spiritual forces of evil in the heavenly realms."

Beloved, God wants you to focus on doing well—no matter what comes your way. As you do that, all the bad things that people do to you, God will take care of them on your behalf. God wants to bring the good spirit deposited in you to destroy the evil that exists in the world. Guard your spirit and don't compete with evil; heap the burning coals over your enemies by being good to them and leave the rest to God.

Prayer of the Day

Dear God, help me control my emotions so that I may be able to act in accordance with your Word at all times. Soften my heart and mind into understanding that revenge comes from you. You know the root cause of every conflict and challenge that I come across. Open my heart to more goodness so that I may act in a manner that pleases you. In Jesus's name. Amen.

9 March

"So likewise shall my Heavenly Father do also unto you, if ye from your hearts forgive not everyone his brother their trespasses (Matthew 18:35, KJV).

Prayer Point

Jesus Christ came from heaven. All He did was tell the truth. He emphasised the importance of forgiveness through the Lord's Prayer and also on the verse above to highlight that when you forgive your brother's sins, you also get your sins forgiven by God.

You can only withhold forgiveness against your brother if you know with absolute certainty that you will never need forgiveness from God—and that is not possible for as long as you live.

Let your prayer today be for you to cover all the wrongs you have suffered from all your relatives or family members. Pray a prayer that releases them from your thoughts as people you could have even classified as your enemies.

10 March

"When Jesus saw their faith, he said to the paralytic, 'Son, your sins are forgiven'" (Mark 2:5, NIV).

Prayer Point

Certain problems in our lives come as a result of disobeying God. It could be that a certain sin in our life opened the door for the evil one to enter and torment your life.

When the paralytic was presented to Jesus, the only thing that Jesus did was tell the paralytic that His sins were forgiven and all was well again. This scripture reveals that some of the problems that we have only require Jesus to forgive us of our sins so that we can become whole again.

Ask God to reveal to you the root cause of some of your challenges in life. Ask for forgiveness, repent of your sins, believe that it shall be well—just like the paralytic in the scripture above—and receive your emotional and physical healing.

11 March

"If your brother sins, rebuke him, and if he repents forgive him. If he sins against you seven times in a day, and seven times comes back to you and says, 'I repent,' forgive him" (Luke 17:3-4, NLT).

Prayer Point

It is every Christian's responsibility to care for one another. If one of us does something that we see will lead to death, we need to get the wisdom from God to rebuke such a person. When the person finds their feet, we forgive them and carry on.

When someone sins against us many times in a day but repents of their sin and asks for forgiveness, our responsibility as children of God is to forgive. The measure of the time we ought to forgive is infinite because we will be wronged and need to forgive for as long as we live.

Pray for God's guidance when you are faced with a brother or sister who has gone astray that you may bring them back to the good way of life through words that will gently rebuke with the intention of correcting the wrong.

12 March

"But he that shall blaspheme against the Holy Ghost hath never forgiveness, but is in danger of eternal damnation" (Mark 3:29, KJV).

Prayer Point

When Lord Jesus performed miracles and got many people healed, some people questioned the authority by that He was performing the miracles and healing the sick. They accused Jesus of being possessed by Beelzebub, prince of demons (John 3:20-28). When He heard this, he spoke to them in parables saying that a Kingdom cannot be divided against itself—and the devil cannot cast his own self. In verse 29, Jesus says that anyone who blasphemes against the Holy Spirit will not be forgiven—that is the only sin that cannot be forgiven.

Often we see many uniquely talented servants of God and we start questioning and doubting the power they use to perform miracles and healing the sick without much evidence or discernment. Questioning and accusing people without proof or through discernment could lead to blaspheming against the Holy Spirit.

Pray unto God to help you not sin against the Holy Spirit. Pray that He shows you what sinning against the Holy Spirit entails so that you can avoid sinning against Him. Ask God to help you grow spiritually so that you can discern the spirits accordingly. Pray about every situation that brings doubt in your life and expect God to reveal the truth.

13 March

"When they kept on questioning him, he straightened up and said to them, 'If any one of you is without sin, let him be the first to throw a stone at her'" (John 8:7, NIV).

Prayer Point

Jesus used powerful words of wisdom to illustrate that forgiveness is very important because there isn't any one of us who has never sinned. In this scripture, He invited any person who felt they did not have a sin to cast a stone on the woman. He said that because He knew all those people had sinned but were quick to judge and punish.

God expects you to have mercy on the people who have wronged you. He expects you to rethink your own sins and weaknesses before you can judge someone and find the person unworthy of receiving your forgiveness.

To forgive is not an easy task because it makes you feel like a loser. However, if you look at it in God's way, forgiveness positions you to receive God's favour with your very own sins. Pray that God helps you not to judge others and punish them—but to make you acknowledge your own weaknesses so that you can easily find it necessary to forgive.

14 March

"Therefore, if you are offering your gift at the altar and there remember that your brother has something against you; leave your gift there in front of the altar. First go and be reconciled to your brother; then come and offer your gift" (Matthew 5:23-24, NIV).

Prayer Point

We often offend each other intentionally or in other ways that give great pain to other people. When you become aware of the fact that you have made someone sad or angry, it becomes your duty to seek peace and forgiveness so that you can be reconciled.

The verse urges us to make peace with whoever we offend before we can make an offering gift to the Lord. God is the God of Peace. He wants us to be able to make peace with everyone who we offend before we can give Him our gifts.

Pray that God helps you whenever you make an offering to God to first identify the people you are not in good standing with so that you can go and ask for their forgiveness and be reconciled to them.

15 March

"There will be no mercy for those who have not shown mercy to others. But if you have been merciful, God will be merciful when he judges you" (James 2:13, NLT).

Forgiveness is being merciful with an understanding and conviction that you as the victim have the potential to wrong others. If you have been merciful to others through forgiveness of sins, God will be merciful to you during judgment.

Mercy is visible when you know you should have been punished but—instead of a punishment—all charges against you were dropped.

I met a woman who grew up as an orphan; she was very smart and got sponsorships to study abroad. She has a PhD and is a very successful businesswoman; she is also a truly committed Christian. Whenever she recalls her childhood, she sees the mercies of God in her life. She has adopted three children as a result of continued gratitude and joy from God. Since God has been graceful to her, she feels she has to give to people in need because God has been merciful to her. She is extending the mercies to other orphans. If she continues living this way, she will be shown mercy in other areas of her life. Matthew 5:7 says, "Blessed are the merciful for they will be shown mercy."

Beloved, forgiveness is of more benefit to you than it is to the other person. You should start viewing forgiveness as something that will benefit you more than others.

I'm sure you know that you reap the fruits of the seed you have planted; if you plant a seed of mercy, you will reap mercy.

Be merciful so that you can receive mercy too; forgive in order to be forgiven by your Father who is in heaven.

Prayer of the Day

Lord Jesus, from today, prepare my heart to plant the seeds of forgiveness and love across all the people that I meet in this lifetime. Help me overcome my shortcomings of not easily letting go so that I may work in your fullness of grace. Remove any trace of resentment in my heart and allow me to understand the principle of reaping what I sow. Direct my hand to only plant the seeds that will bear good fruit.

16 March

"Yes, God does these things again and again for people" (Job 33:29, NLT).

Prayer Point

God is truly a God of second chances. Even when you sin and go back to Him to ask for forgiveness, He gives you a chance to start all over. He does not recall the mistakes you have made in the past because He knows the hidden treasures in you that will manifest the second time around.

Sometimes people may stumble along the way, but God is always there to give you another chance to allow you to grow so that you don't repeat your mistakes—and you get to teach others to be vigilant when approaching the pit.

Beloved, God is waiting for you to get up on areas that you had given up because you felt a sense of hopelessness. He is saying to you that He is still willing to give you another chance to try again. All you need to do is to take Him at His Word; His Word never fails.

17 March

"Judge not, and ye shall not be judged: condemn not, and ye shall not be condemned: forgive, and ye shall be forgiven" (Luke 6:37, ESV).

Prayer Point

It is easy to fall into a trap of judging someone and putting a sentence to the person that you may deem appropriate. Sometimes when someone has upset you, it may look legitimate to refuse to talk to them because you want the person to feel that they have truly hurt you.

According to the Word of God, what you give is what you get; if you spend a lot of time finding fault with others and magnifying their weaknesses, God will find a more valid reason to do the same with you.

Let your focus today be a prayer that sets your mind free from judging and condemning others. Instead, pray for a heart that will be so full of love and forgiveness toward other people who have wronged you.

18 March

"And the prayer of faith shall save the sick, and the Lord shall raise him up; and if he have committed sins, they shall be forgiven him" (James 5:15, KJV).

Prayer Point

To have faith in God means believing His Word as it stands in the Bible. Complete faith in God means there is no area in your life where you trust God the least. Believe that God can turn things around for your own good in all areas of your life.

A prayer that is done by faith to God will make everything that was not well in terms of sickness to be healed and to have the forgiveness of sins. God is not waiting for you to make a mistake and then he will punish you. He is interested in how much you grow spiritually.

Increase your faith through regular fasting and prayer. For any difficult situation or problem, approach the throne of grace through faith, believing God. Invite others to pray with you so that you can be lifted up in prayer

19 March

"If we confess our sins, he is faithful and just to forgive us our sins, and to cleanse us from all unrighteousness" (1 John 1:9, KJV).

Prayer Point

The process for our sins to be forgiven starts with a confession of our sins. Confession is acknowledging the mistakes you have made and then asking God to forgive us.

In every moment of our lives, we are faced with different temptations that can cause us to sin. These temptations can be in the form of prospective financial gain or other temporary worldly pleasures. It is important to remember that God is waiting for us to name our sins and confess them all to him. He is faithful and just to forgive us. God knows our weaknesses and He is willing to help us overcome them and cleanse us of unrighteousness.

Today, make a prayer of confession for all your sins—especially the ones you have been concealing (thinking that God is not noticing). Ask God to help you reclaim a righteous life in Christ Jesus.

20 March

"Whosoever therefore shall confess me before men, him will I confess also before my Father that is in heaven" (Matthew 10:32, KJV).

Prayer Point

When you confess Jesus, you speak openly about Him without restrictions because you know who He is in your life. It must not be only when you go to church that you get to talk about Him. Even when you are at work or with some of your friends, don't be ashamed to talk about Him. If you openly confess Jesus before men, He promises to confess you before God in heaven.

There are many traditions in different cultures all over the world. Some Christians are from families that are not saved. As a result, they still practice certain traditions that require every family member to adhere to—even if they are not in line with the Christian belief. If you are a Christian, don't conform to practices that are not in line with the Scripture. Confess your Lord and Saviour Jesus—and don't be ashamed of saying that Jesus is your Saviour.

Allow the light of God to shine through you when you pray, when you talk to other people, and when you work. Confess the name of Jesus when you pray in public. When you confess the name of Jesus, He will also confess you before God.

21 March

"Blessed are they whose iniquities are forgiven, and whose sins are covered" (Romans 4:7, KJV).

Prayer Point

When you commit iniquity, you have failed to demonstrate at least a single Christian moral value. You are operating under the influence of the enemy. God still has mercy to forgive the most terrible of sins because all sins have been forgiven through the blood of Jesus.

As you pray today, pray that God forgives you of the sins you have committed with your thoughts—those sins that only you know you have committed. Pray for other people in your family, church, colleagues, and any other person who comes to mind. I invite you to confess all your sins and renounce any iniquity in your life so that you can now live a new life of hope and peace in Christ Jesus.

22 March

"And when you stand praying, if you hold anything against anyone, forgive him, so that your father in heaven may forgive you your sins (Mark 11:25, NIV).

When I was a little girl, I used to enjoy holding grudges on people who upset me. I would sulk and refuse to talk to them until I felt I had punished them enough. This would also happen when my mom made me angry. I would sometimes refuse to eat; my mother would give my food to one of my siblings. When she did that I would feel like exploding. I did all that because I wanted my mom to see that she had angered me. I was the one who would be hurt the most because I would refuse to eat the food because of pride. It would kill me inside to see my food given to someone else.

As I became older and spent more time in God's Word, I realized that resentment is a strategy that the devil uses to deceive us into thinking that we are entitled to hold the grudge. Someone said, "Resentment is like drinking poison, hoping that your enemy will die from it." The longer you hold the grudge, the more deprived you get by not talking to those people who have angered you because you still want to make the point that someone has angered you.

When you pray, it's important to recall and forgive all the people who have wronged us so that our Father can also forgive us our trespasses. It may not be easy to forgive, but a lot of practice that goes with it. It becomes a necessary habit to develop as a Christian. To forgive opens up God's heart for Him to be able to forgive us.

When you have forgiven someone, you feel free. It is as if some heavy burden has been taken off your shoulders. Sometimes we get it all wrong by thinking that when we forgive, we lose ground. When you forgive, you take a step closer to getting to God and having him forgive your sins. Some circumstances and sickness around us are as a result of resentment. If only we could forgive them, we could get well and be set free.

Prayer of the Day

Dear God, thank you for revealing to me the most powerful weapon in my Christian faith that is the requirement to forgive others so that you can forgive me. Teach me to view others more important than me so that I can see them to have the same needs as mine that are to have their sins forgiven as mine.

23 March

"And be ye kind one to another, tender hearted, forgiving one another, even as God for Christ's sake hath forgiven you" (Ephesians 4:32, KJV).

Prayer Point

Forgiving someone for something small can be easy. However, forgiving someone for something big like having murdered your loved ones can be very difficult and could take a while. It becomes difficult when we try to do it our own way and not God's way.

Forgiveness of sins God's way will be in the form of trying to understand from the other person's point of view in terms of what went wrong on their side. Kindness and love for other people should be good enough to equip you to overcome any pain in your way. Ask the Holy Spirit to help you speak to others in kindness and love.

24 March

"Do not judge by appearances, but judge with right judgment" (John 7:24, ESV).

Prayer Point

When in a state of being unable to understand what went wrong that led to someone hurting us and make us feel so unworthy of better treatment, we often judge based on what we see in the flesh and not the supernatural.

Sometimes people hurt each other physically and emotionally. It may not be based on something physically, but it can be based on something spiritually. An evil spirit can take over a person's life in order to manipulate the person into committing sin.

The scripture cautions us not to judge by appearances because things are not always the way they seem. It is only with the ability to discern spiritually that God can reveal to us the underlying cause of the problem. As you pray today, ask God to help you stay away from judging others—but discern the source of their actions that cause you pain.

25 March

"There is only one Lawgiver and Judge, the one who is able to save and destroy. But you—who are you to judge your neighbour?" (James 4:12, NIV).

Prayer Point

God is the only one who can judge because He has all the facts. He knows the hidden influences in every person's life that make people behave in a certain way. He even knows the most appropriate measure for punishment when someone has sinned.

When we get to heaven by God's grace, we will be shocked to see people we have judged to be sinners receiving God's pardon because certain actions people commit are beyond their control. Some are not innocent, but God knows the root of every problem. Beloved, your responsibility is to love your neighbour and not to judge them because God has the ultimate authority for every human being.

As you pray, make it a habit to ask God to deliver you from the sin of judging others so that you can forgive everyone who seeks your forgiveness. Pray that God deals with everyone who offends you in the way that He deems suitable.

26 March

"Do not let any unwholesome talk come out of your mouths, but only what is helpful for building others up according to their needs, that it may benefit those who listen" (Ephesians 4:29).

Prayer Point

When resentment rules your life, it becomes difficult to have positive things to say about other people. Your mind grows accustomed to looking at faults in every person. Whatever you say about the people who have offended you, becomes unwholesome.

Scripture urges every believer to say good things when we talk. You can only say good things if only good things are stored inside your heart. A forgiving heart will enable you to share the benefits of forgiveness with other people who could be battling within this area.

God expects us to be role models by storing and sharing good news with our mouths for the benefit of every person that we come across so that they benefit something from us. We can only do that if we let go of bitterness in our hearts and substitute it with goodness that comes from God.

27 March

"Do to others as you would have them do to you" (Luke 6:31, NIV).

Prayer Point

What you would like to receive from others should be the same as what you give them. In essence, there should be no double standards. It would be unfair to expect to be forgiven by others if you cherish holding grudges and don't want to let go of bitterness.

If you have a problem with forgiving others, you should not have a problem when other people don't want to forgive you because that would be what you practice. This verse is full of wisdom because it deals with our weaknesses that make us live a life that only wants to receive the best—but it cannot give the best.

As you pray today, ask the mercies for God to shine through your spiritual eyes that you will start to cultivate a life of fairness in all areas of your life. Deep down, you know that you want the best to come your way. As a start of a new season in your life, be prepared to give the best in order to receive the best. In other words, be prepared to forgive in order to receive forgiveness.

28 March

"Brothers and sisters, if someone is caught in a sin, you who live by the Spirit should restore that person gently. But watch yourselves, or you also may be tempted" (Galatians 6:1, NIV).

Prayer Point

Temptation often can often cause a child of God to go astray. It can happen that one of your loved ones starts to abuse alcohol and starts to become violent and ends up beating you or forcing you to react by fighting back instead of seeking amicable ways to restore the person and forgiving them of any wrongdoing.

God has entrusted you with a responsibility to not respond to people who have gone astray in an ungodly manner. He expects us to gently pray for the restoration of that person's soul. Fighting back a person who hurt us is not in accordance with what God expects us to do.

It is my prayer that God can guide you throughout your Christian journey to be in a position where you can love other people and remember that God created all of us. He loves us all and your role is to continue in God's love.

29 March

"But as for you, ye thought evil against me; but God meant it unto good, to bring to pass, as it is this day, to save much people alive. Now therefore fear ye not: I will nourish you, and your little ones. And he comforted them, and spake kindly unto them" (Genesis 50:20-21, KJV).

Prayer Point

Joseph's brothers were very jealous and thought of killing him, but later they decided to sell him to the Egyptians. He was highly favoured by His father and that made his brothers very jealous. Later, when Joseph introduced himself to his brothers, they became scared because they were thinking that Joseph would pay revenge for what they once did to Him—but Joseph chose to forgive them.

What Joseph's brothers meant for the worst, God turned it for the good because even though they sold Him with bad intentions God had a better plan for Joseph to save people.

Your responsibility toward family or friends who have treated you unfairly or were jealous of you is to forgive them and love them. All you need to do is release them because what they intended for the worst, God will turn around for your own good. If you are constantly unhappy at work because people are treating you unfairly and you feel compelled to leave your job in order to start your own business, God will bless that business and move you from a position of just being an ordinary employee to a successful CEO. Your blessings are not dependent on the favour you receive from men but on the favour you receive from God.

30 March

"Therefore is the kingdom of heaven likened unto a certain king that would take account of his servants. And when he had begun to reckon, one was brought unto him that owed him ten thousand talents. But forasmuch as he had not to pay, his lord commanded him to be sold, and his wife, and children, and all that he had, and payment to be made. The servant therefore fell down, and worshipped him, saying, Lord, have patience with me, and I will pay thee all. Then the lord of that servant was moved with compassion, and loosed him, and forgave him the debt" (Matthew 18:23–35, KJV).

Prayer Point

This scripture illustrates the mercy that God has for us. He is often moved with compassion to forgive of our sins. There are things that we owe God; it could be that we don't pray enough. We don't use enough of the gifts that He has blessed us with, but we each owe God something. When we pray, we ought to ask for forgiveness of sins.

The servant humbled himself and started worshipping God and begging the Lord for His patience and promised to pay the master what he owed. The Lord forgave his debt without conditions.

You need forgiveness more than what you need to get back from the people who have wronged you. God is awaiting your plea to be forgiven and He is ready to grant you. Release all the people who have wronged you in the past and receive forgiveness from God.

31 March

"Dearly beloved, avenge not yourselves, but rather give place unto wrath: for it is written, Vengeance is mine; I will repay, saith the Lord" (Romans 12:19, KJV).

Prayer Point

When someone slaps you in the face, the natural reaction is to immediately slap them back even harder if you can so that you can show your enemy how angry you are and how hard you can pay back with another slap. There are many things that get us upset on a daily basis; sometimes we feel forgiving and starting a new chapter will not do, but we just want to teach someone a lesson or two by paying revenge.

God says we should not avenge ourselves, but we ought to have room for anger for vengeance is the Lord's and He will repay on your behalf. When the Lord repays for all the hurt and suffering that you had endured, He does it well.

Our enemies will laugh at our misfortune, but instead of us wishing them double our misfortune, let us allow God to avenge on our behalf. Take those people who have stolen our self-esteem and made false accusations unto the Lord in prayer. He will repay because vengeance is His; our responsibility is to forgive.

Chapter 4

Be Courageous
Because God Is With You

1 April

"Moses said to God, 'Who am I that I should go to Pharaoh and bring the Israelites out of Egypt?' And God said, 'I will be with you. And this will be the sign to you that it is I who have sent you: When you have brought the people out of Egypt, you will worship God on this mountain'" (Exodus 3:11-12, NIV).

Can you recall the times you had to do something and felt you couldn't because you felt you did not have what it takes to do the task? This happens to many people and it becomes more complicated when God asks you to do something.

When God spoke to Moses, He was giving Moses an instruction to bring the children of Israel out of Egypt, but Moses did not feel He was the right person to do the job. This response that Moses gave to God is very typical of many people's response—me included. Moses was afraid of Pharaoh and very reluctant to go. Fear normally comes in as a result of lack of faith. For a second, Moses forgot who was giving him the instruction. If he had fully remembered who he was talking to, he would have realised that he had nothing to be afraid of since everything will be taken care of by God. Fear takes over when we rely on our own strengths and see them as inadequate—and when we consider our weaknesses to be so many that they limit us. However, when we believe in God for every situation, we believe in the power of someone greater than us. When you believe that God will always be with you, nothing will scare or intimidate you.

After reading these verses, reflect on your life and the things that God is instructing you to do. Examine your heart and see if fear is a hindrance to your stepping forward. God will not ask you to do something out of your own strength or ability because He knows that you have limitations. God will be with you just as He was with Moses. All you need to do is to trust in Him to carry you through.

You may be placed in a situation where you are the only born-again Christian in your family and you are scared to talk to your family members about God. He will be with you—don't trust your own strength. Trust in Him for His power is not limited; He will help you convey the good news to your family, but He needs to do that through you. God gives us the power to do things that He wants us to do by working through us. God gives us the power to overcome through His spirit (John 4:24).

No matter how big and scary the assignment that God wants you to do is, He will be with you just as he promised to be with Moses.

Prayer of the Day

Dear Heavenly Father, I ask you to help me to fully trust in you in whatever task I embark upon. Eliminate all the fear in my heart and fill my heart with your love and your presence so that I can be reminded always of your power. Be visible, Lord, in every aspect of my life. Talk to me in ways that will enable me to identify your voice and listen. I want to trust you with my whole life from now on, in Jesus's name. Amen.

2 April

"David also said to Solomon his son, 'Be strong and courageous, and do the work. Do not be afraid or discouraged, for the Lord God, my God, is with you. He will not fail you or forsake you until all the work for the service of the temple of the Lord is finished'" (1 Chronicles 28:20, NIV).

Prayer Point

David lived his life knowing God and he had the experience of God's power and mercies. He believed that a requirement for God to use someone requires strength, courage, and action—God will do the rest.

You could have been procrastinating on a lot of tasks because you felt inadequate to complete the tasks. Have the strength and the courage and believe that God is with you and He will be with you until what He has planted in your heart is complete.

3 April

"When I am afraid, I will trust in you. In God, whose Word I praise, in God I trust; I will not be afraid. What can mortal man do to me?" (Psalm 56:3-4, NIV).

Prayer Point

When fear rules in one's heart, the devil throws different options that he knows will lead you in trouble. When you are waiting to write an exam and you are unsure of how you will handle it, the thoughts of cancelling the exam or sneaking some notes to copy from during the exam may come up.

When you are uncertain and afraid, that is the time for you to trust in God even more and ask for His protection. God is not limited by space or distance. He is not afraid of any human being.

Let go of the fear of the terrible circumstances in your heart and allow the love and peace of God to control you. Continue to trust in God for victory. Pray for the spirit of fear to be removed so that you may continue trusting in God.

4 April

"For I am the Lord, your God, who takes hold of your right hand and says to you, Do not fear; I will help you" (Isaiah 41:13, NIV).

Prayer Point

God knows about our insecurities. He knows men's fears because men started becoming afraid when they committed sin in the Garden of Eden. The initial fear was felt by Adam when he disobeyed God.

Through Jesus, we are saved by God's grace and we are protected by His blood. We are now on God's right hand through Jesus and God is always on our side and protecting us. God wants us to shake off any form of fear and doubt and help us to be courageous for He is there to help us with our needs.

Acknowledge your lack of power to do anything but submit to God's power in your life. Lean on God for strength and courage and He will pull you through. Let your prayer today include yielding to God for strength and courage.

5 April

"Therefore do not fear them. For there is nothing concealed that will not be revealed, or hidden that will not be known" (Matthew 10:26).

Prayer Point

I knew of a man who was mightily feared by people who lived close to his home. This man was not violent or cruel in any way, but he possessed a strange presence that made people feel uncomfortable around him. It was as if he possessed certain powers that people could not clearly define or get accustomed to.

We should fear the Lord at all times because the person you fear the most has the power to influence your actions—and even some of the decisions that you must make.

Let no circumstance scare you to the point that you cannot pray. Rebuke the spirit of fear in your life in the name of Jesus for there is no name above the name of Jesus. Pray that anything planned in darkness to destroy you be revealed and broken in the name of Jesus.

6 April

"For ye have not received the spirit of bondage again to fear; but ye have received the Spirit of adoption, whereby we cry, Abba, Father" (Romans 8:15, KJV).

Prayer Point

God has given us the spirit of acceptance where we should not feel condemned. God is concerned with how we look from the inside out.

He knows that it is only who we are that will be taken to heaven when we pass on. God has not given us the spirit of fear because fear is a form of bondage—but He has given us love and the spirit of acceptance.

You could have lived your life without a father figure or you could have had a father who did not play his role and was never there for you. Be at peace to know that God is the role model that you need for He never changes. He is a father to the fatherless (Psalm 68:5).

Pray and cry to Abba Father to receive the Holy Spirit that accepts you into God's Kingdom and sets you free. Pray for all existing doubt in your life to be replaced by faith in God because doubt does not come from God.

7 April

"Keep your lives free from the love of money and be content with what you have, because God has said, never will I leave you, never will I forsake you. So we say with confidence, The Lord is my helper; I will not be afraid. What can man do to me?" (Hebrews 13:5-6, NIV).

Prayer Point

When your life is in order and you know that you are doing everything to please God, then God will be there to help and protect you. You could be working on a difficult project, but when God is your helper, He will send the right people to come your way and help you with it. He will remove all the complexity that surrounds the work and make you prosperous.

God is more powerful than we can ever imagine. Don't look at the challenges that are intimidating you in your life right now; focus on receiving the breakthrough to overcome through God.

God will never leave you or forsake you. He is interested in getting you through the most difficult circumstances and seeing you prosper and moving from strength to strength in faith.

8 April

"It is good for me that I have been afflicted, that I may learn your statutes" (Psalm 119:71, ESV).

While undergoing a trial, we may not fully understand why we have to undergo so much pain. Most of the time, hardships make us question God and wonder why they are happening. This is due to our lack of understanding of how God expects us to grow in terms of our character. Our character has to resemble Christ's character.

When undergoing affliction, it is important to see what the affliction has taught us. In many cases, trials have a lot to teach us. Sometime we get to experience rejection at a young age so that we can learn to love and appreciate others and those people we come across later in life.

I knew of a wealthy man who loved God so much. This man had everything going for Him; his marriage was intact and his businesses were prospering. He was in good health and one would safely say that life was going well until he had an accident and had to undergo surgeries. He started to realise that there was another side to life. One thing that this man did was to continue thanking God for everything—even his affliction because he felt that even though he was in pain, God used the affliction to remind him that he needed him in good times or bad times.

Very few people could think like this man when being afflicted. It is when we are afflicted that we wonder why all the hurt and disappointment is happening to us and not to the person next door. The answer is simple: the person next door is as important as you are and you are no exception to anything that is happening around the world. Sometimes affliction is there to teach us to love unconditionally and to forgive.

My prayer for you as you read this message is for God to sustain you after every pain and, most importantly, for God to reveal the lesson behind every affliction that you face. There is a lesson and that lesson has to do with what God expects you to know and cling to based on His commands. The psalmist is acknowledging the affliction of the trial because something good happened—that was to learn God's ways.

Whenever you face trials, know that God has intended it for your good. Just exercise patience because when it is over, you will marvel at the goodness of God throughout the trial.

Prayer of the Day

Dear God, I know that sometimes I question your love for me—especially when undergoing physical and emotional pain. Thank you for teaching me that affliction is necessary so that I may know your ways and live in accordance with your statutes. Lord, I know that your love for me is deeper than what I can see from the surface. Teach me, Lord, to appreciate your love for me even more—even if I don't feel your love at that moment.

9 April

"God is our refuge and strength, a very present help in trouble" (Psalms 46:1, NIV).

Prayer Point

Have you ever been in trouble and felt helpless because you wanted someone to help you but no one was there to assist you? I'm sure almost every person falls into trouble once in a while. When you look around, you feel so depressed that no one is there to help you get out of trouble. When Shadrach, Meshach, and Abednego refused to worship the idols, they were thrown into the fiery furnace, but they did not burn because God rescued them (Daniel 3:1-27).

God is our place of safety; he is always willing to protect you and give you strength to continue on your journey of life. He is always present for anyone who seeks Him for protection in all walks of life.

People can fail you at times—even your kids or relatives—because they do not have the capability that God has to protect His creation from all sorts of trouble. God is always there to protect you. Pray for His help in times of trouble and receive His help.

10 April

"Seek Yahweh and his strength. Seek his face forevermore" (1 Chronicles 16:11, WEB).

Prayer Point

Yahweh is another name for God. In my childhood, I would sometimes wonder why it was necessary for me to pray to God if He could read my mind and see what I needed. God is the King and He must be sought for His strength and power.

God is there to be honoured by us and not the other way round. We have to seek His face to show that we need Him to solve our situations. The more we seek Him, the more we show Him how serious we are to get solutions to move forward.

Pray and seek the face of God and His strength so that your needs can be met through His strength. The more you seek, the more serious you are about your situation. Pray that God gives you the ability to withstand hardships and that you may continue doing good in all circumstances through His strength.

11 April

"He gives power to the faint, and to him who has no might he increases strength" (Isaiah 40:29, ESV).

Prayer Point

Our Lord knows that our journey on earth will consists of good times and the bad times, but the time that calls for us to seek help and encouragement is not when all is well—but when something in our life has been destabilised. At times, we become weak along the journey and God knows that we need to top up our strength.

God awaits us to ask for strength from Him in order to progress because He has the power to increase the strength. We don't need to rely on our own strength—we need to rely on His strength in order to be lifted emotionally.

Pray for the people around you who have experienced some challenges lately so that God can give them the strength to carry on. Some could be on the verge of giving up because they don't know where they can get the strength from; stand in the gap for them so that God can increase their strength.

12 April

"I sought the Lord, and He heard me, And delivered me from all my fears" (Psalm 34:4, KJV).

Prayer Point

Imagine calling someone's name loudly until you get their attention. The psalmist must have had a similar encounter of seeking the Lord until he was heard because God heard his cry and He answered. He did not just seek the Lord for nothing; he sought the Lord for deliverance.

You may need to seek the Lord to come to your rescue from a difficult circumstance that you could be facing. There are different forms of bondage that we find ourselves in; some people are born in families that suffer from illnesses that have been running from generation to generation—and such conditions need to be prayed for in order to be delivered. You need to seek the Lord and ask God to deliver you from bondage.

Call upon the Lord when in trouble. Cry out to him in prayer and let your voice be heard. He will never turn a deaf ear from you. He will give you the strength to carry on. Even when you face false accusations, He will always be there to present and defend your case.

13 April

"My flesh and my heart fail, but God is the strength of my heart and my portion forever" (Psalms 73:26, NIV).

Prayer Point

Youth have different concerns in life compared to older people because they see the world through the lens of a young generation. Everything seems possible when you are young because physically you are strong and can become an athlete and do lots of things. When you get older, you start to realise that you cannot rely on your physical strength because that starts to gradually fail.

Getting old opens your heart to reality because you start to appreciate your youth and you realize that your youth is not a product of what you worked for—it was because of the grace of the Lord. The psalmist acknowledged that when his flesh and heart fails, God will be all that he needs.

Let the Holy Spirit teach you to wait upon the Lord for strength and courage, knowing that God will never fail you. Let Him strengthen your heart and give you the courage that you need.

14 April

"Now to him who is able to do exceedingly abundantly above all that we ask or think, according to the power that works in us" (Ephesians 3:20, AKJV).

Prayer Point

The power that we have as human beings is limited and can only do so much. Without the help of God, we cannot do anything. We cannot activate the spirit within us to carry us around, but God is able to do exceedingly abundantly above all.

You could be having a vision of your life, but that vision can only be accomplished through Christ who does exceedingly abundantly with no limitations. All you need to have done is to have visualized that something and draw from God for the power to bring it into existence.

Seek the Lord in prayer and meditation on His Word to activate the power of God inside you. God does not want to work around you; He wants to work through you and do extraordinary things in your life.

15 April

"And not only so, but we glory in tribulations also: knowing that tribulation worketh patience; And patience, experience; and experience, hope" (Romans 5:3-4, KJV).

When bad things happen to us, we may not feel happy. However, there is a reason why the Bible says we should be joyful when tribulations come our way. There is always power in tribulations because they unlock blessings if we continue obeying God. Tribulations can be a disguised way of getting a blessing, but the result will be determined by how we respond to the tribulation at that time.

Life is like embarking on a journey of uncertainty. No one knows how your journey will unfold; we don't even know what we will experience or how heavy or enjoyable those experiences will be.

However, we know that God knows everything about our lives from start to finish.

Perseverance can be difficult when facing hardships because, in some of the challenges, giving up may seem to be the quickest and easiest route—even though giving up is not the best option. Our focus should always be to persevere in hardships through the Holy Spirit. The strength to persevere comes from God as it manifests through the complete work of the Holy Spirit in us.

God wants you to be joyful at all times. Remember that God's plan is to prosper you and not to harm you. God is interested in your true love for him and how you grow and mature for His purposes.

Prayer of the Day

Teach me, Lord, to persevere when faced with challenges or tribulations. Help me focus all my strength on you in times of hardships so that I may draw courage from you so that my character can take the necessary shape that will be more aligned to the ways and the will of my Lord and Saviour's Jesus Christ. Amen.

16 April

"Do not let this Book of the Law depart from your mouth; meditate on it on it day and night, so that you may be careful to do everything written in it. Then you will be prosperous and successful" (Joshua 1:8, NIV).

Prayer Point

Proverbs 18:21 says that death and life are in the power of the tongue—and those who love it will eat its fruit. When you set aside time to meditate on the Word of God, you are planting life in your heart. You will speak life because you will be careful to do everything that is written in the Bible.

Meditation is a very powerful method to train the mind because it allows the Word of God to sink deep inside you. It transforms your whole thinking and aligns it to God's thinking. Meditation helps you remember God's statutes and to live by them.

Pray that God grants you understanding as you start reading and dwelling in His Word as often as you can so that your mind and actions can be transformed by the knowledge, wisdom, and revelation that will flow from God's word.

17 April

"No one will be able to stand against you as long as you live. For I will be with you as I was with Moses. I will not fail you or abandon you. Be strong and courageous, for you are the one who will lead these people to possess all the land I swore to their ancestors I would give them" (Joshua 1:5-6, NLT).

Prayer Point

When God is on your side, all things are possible. When Joshua took over from Moses, God gave Joshua the strength, wisdom, and assurance to carry on the work that was set for him to lead God's people. God has never told His servants to be afraid; He always said be strong and courageous. That has to do with an attitude change that He required His servants to have for He knew that He would do the rest of the work.

When God promises something, He sees it to completion. You could be faced with making important decisions that could have your life positioned for great success. Fear of the unknown and doubt make you procrastinate and abandon your plans because you are afraid of failure before you even start.

Any thinking that limits your progress is not from God—but from the adversary because he wants to limit you. Let God help you with your weaknesses for His strength is demonstrated through your weaknesses. Be strong in every situation and trust Him to use you to take your church, family, or country to the Promised Land.

18 April

"My soul is weary with sorrow: strengthen me according to your Word" (Psalms 119:28, NIV).

Prayer Point

God used to speak to His people or convey messages to his people through His prophets. In the Old Testament, He would often bring messages of encouragement through Moses, Joshua, or Elijah.

In the present day, God speaks to us through His prophets, but the main one He speaks through is His word. It is normal to feel sad sometimes and want to hear from God so that your spirit will be lifted.

God knows our needs; when we are down and don't know how to get up, God strengthens us through His Word. We can only hear from God if we are listening to Him and we are expecting a breakthrough from God. Pray that God directs you to His Word; that will encourage you and give you more strength when your spirit is low.

19 April

"The Lord is my light and my salvation; whom shall I fear? The Lord is the strength of my life; of whom shall I be afraid?" (Psalm 27:1, AKJV).

Prayer Point

Because God is your light and your salvation, anything that has been hidden in the darkness in your life will be brought to light. As everything in your life that was previously in the dark is revealed by the light, you will have nothing to fear.

Open up your heart to God for the light of God to shine through. Don't leave any room in your heart for darkness to prevail. God wants to light up everything to cast out all the fear in you. He can only do that if you open up your whole heart to Him. God is a jealous God (Deuteronomy 6:15) who only wants you for Himself.

Jesus has authority on earth and in heaven. Have faith in Him and let go of all the fear in your heart. Allow God's light to shine through you and cast away everything that is not of God in Jesus's name.

20 April

"So do not fear, for I am with you; do not be dismayed, for I am your God. I will strengthen you and help you; I will uphold you with my righteous right hand" (Isaiah 41:10, NIV).

Prayer Point

God has said, "Do not fear!" to different people because he knew that, with fear operating in a person's mind, there is nothing that a person can accomplish. "For God hath not given us the spirit of fear; but of power, and of love, and of a sound mind" (2 Timothy 1:7). Fear is a spirit that definitely does not come from God.

Just as God has said to His servants that they must not fear, He is telling you to never be afraid of anything for He will strengthen you. God expects you to let go of the spirit of fear and allow Him to step into your life so that He can strengthen you and meet your needs.

God knows that you need His help and He is there to hold you with His hand to help you accomplish the things that He has intended for you to accomplish. Trust in God for new strength in your life for He is promising to uphold you with His hand so that you can be victorious.

21 April

"Do not be afraid; you will not suffer shame. Do not fear disgrace; you will not be humiliated. You will forget the shame of your youth and remember no more the reproach of your widowhood" (Isaiah 54:4, NIV).

Prayer Point

There are different ways that fear presents itself. Sometimes it presents itself with thoughts that are limiting for example it can make you ask questions such as : "Who do you think you are that you can stand in front of people and proclaim God's word?" When you start assessing yourself and focus on your inadequacies, you won't move forward.

Another form of fear is asking what will happen if you don't succeed and wondering what people will say if you fail. Realize that people will have something to say all the time—whether you make it or you don't—but remember that you were not created by people. You were created by God for His purpose—do not fear.

In order for God to bless you, He does not look at your family background or how good looking you are. "But the Lord said to Samuel, 'Do not look on his appearance or on the height of his stature, because I have rejected him.' For the Lord sees not as man sees: man looks on the outward appearance, but the Lord looks on the heart" (1 Samuel 16:7). Pray that your focus be on God so that you can prosper in the things that you do.

22 April

"Finally, be strong in the Lord and in His mighty power. Put on the full armour of God so that you can take your stand against the devil's schemes. For our struggle is not against flesh and blood, but against the rulers, against the authorities, against the powers of this dark world, and against the spiritual forces of evil in the heavenly realms (Ephesians 6:10-12, NIV).

As a Christian, remember that you are at war. This war manifests in different forms; to some Christians, they are always sick, some are accident prone, some have lost loved ones, some face hatred without having done anything wrong to anyone, some just don't seem to have anything going their way in relationships or careers. Yet, all this can be very hard and difficult to cope with, but you need to remember that you are at war and God is on your side.

The enemy opposes everyone who does good and is of God. The enemy came to steal, kill, and destroy (John 10:10), but Jesus came to give us life and life in abundance. The enemy is after Christians because He knows they do not belong to him. He will always torment you so that you lose focus and not do what God has created you to do. The enemy does not give up easily; you need to persistently pray and resist the devil. He will flee from you. As a child of God, you must rise up against whatever negative circumstance that the enemy is throwing at you and fully depend on the mighty power of Jesus Christ.

Allow God to make you strong through his power. Let the Lord remove all the fear and clothe you with boldness from above. Putting on the armour of God as a child of God means you need to be clothed with the Word of God. That has to be coupled with faith and prayer. I have come across situations where I would be praying and fasting for something and I would experience rejection by some of my friends or from some of the people that I am used to without knowing the cause. I have learnt that instead of judging them, I should turn to God through prayer because Satan uses anyone close to you to attack you. In certain circumstances, the enemy uses your own brother against you—just like what Cain did to Abel. Sometimes he uses even your parents to cause you pain. When people close to us start causing us pain, we need to see beyond the pain we are experiencing and remember the war we are in.

When a soldier goes to a fight—no matter how brave he is—he takes his shield as a protective cover. The same applies to us—as Christians, we need be clothed with the Word of God and have the faith in Jesus so that we can be protected. The Word of God (Ephesians 6:17) brings life and hope to you as a child of God.

Prayer of the Day

Dear Heavenly Father, thank you for reminding me to dwell in your Word and to have faith in you. Lord, all the power resides in you. I am so grateful to be your child because I know that I possess your power through calling out the name of my Lord and Saviour, Jesus Christ of Nazareth. Continue ministering your expectations to me through your word. Guide me and make me understand that I'm not here to fight the flesh and blood. I am here to fight against the spiritual things that may manifest physically without me understanding. Help me stay alert, Mighty God, in Jesus's name. Amen.

23 April

"And do not fear those who kill the body but cannot kill the soul. Rather fear him who can destroy both soul and body in hell: (Matthew 10:28, ESV).

Prayer Point

God has the power to create and to destroy. The enemy has limited power to destroy what God has created—that is the reason there are many deaths in the world today where people kill each other and others die of illnesses. Physical death does not compare to the ultimate death of the soul that will be destroyed in hell by God.

The devil likes putting scary masks on the body to hide his insecurities because he knows he is operating on temporary power to destroy. The Word of God tells us that we must not fear those who kill the body but cannot kill the soul; instead, fear the Lord who has the power to destroy both spirit and body.

Pray always as you grieve your loved ones, thanking God for their lives—no matter how short it could have been. Physical death does not mean eternal death—as long as we continue pursuing Christ through our actions.

24 April

"Be on your guard; stand firm in the faith; be men of courage; be strong" (1 Corinthians 16:13, NIV).

Prayer Point

As Christians, our lives should consist of continuous prayer and being watchful at all times so that we don't get attacked. Imagine a store that sells expensive goods in a place that is known to be surrounded by thieves. If that store is not guarded, the thieves can steal at any time.

God expects us to be watchful so that the enemy does not steal, kill, or destroy anything that belongs to us. Sometimes the things that we lose in our lives were not meant for us to lose; however, because we fail to stay on guard and become too lazy to pray, we lose out.

Get into the habit of praying always and asking the Holy Spirit to direct you to pray for the things that matter in your life at that moment. Refuse to lose your blessings out of neglecting spending time with God through prayer.

25 April

"There is no fear in love. But perfect love drives out fear, because fear has to do with punishment. The one who fears is not made perfect in love" (1 John 4:18, NIV).

Prayer Point

God requires us to love one another as He has loved us because He knows that where love is, there is no hatred, envy, or jealousy. There is only understanding and harmony. Where there is love, there is no fear because when perfect love is present, fear is driven out.

Perfect love comes from God and goes with faith in God. When you have faith in God, you will not fear anything. Fear is another form of bondage that stops a person from living freely.

Trust God to keep all His promises. He will never let you down. He is a faithful God who keeps covenant with all those who trust in Him. Fear God and have complete faith in Him for He will see you through.

26 April

"Know therefore that the Lord your God is God; he is the faithful God, keeping his covenant of love to a thousand generations of those who love him and keep his commands" (Deuteronomy 7:9, NIV).

Prayer Point

God has been faithful from the beginning and He is faithful until the end. He keeps His promises and mercy for all people who love Him. The only way that God sees our love for Him is by how we obey His commands in His word.

Pray that God helps you remain faithful like He is—and to live your life in accordance with the way He would like you to live and to keep His commands. Believe that He will carry you through and make you succeed in all that you do.

Let the Holy Spirit liberate your whole being so that you may have complete faith in God. Pray for the spirit of self-control so that you can be convicted when you begin to go astray in your Christian walk.

27 April

"The Lord is my rock and my fortress and my deliverer, my God, my rock, in whom I take refuge, my shield, and the horn of my salvation, my stronghold" (Psalm 18:2, ESV).

Prayer Point

The Lord will forever be your rock, He will always be there to protect you and be your stronghold. God has an expectation from us in everything that He does for us that has to do with our faith in Him.

There are certain things that can offer us temporary protection, but God's protection is permanent and cannot be made by men. When God delivers you, He lets go of everything that was not good for you.

Invite God to be always your rock, fortress, and deliverer. Ask Him to increase your strength to own your whole being, your thoughts, and to control your mind. Trust in God in all circumstances—even when storms seem strong. Hide under Him for He is your strong shield. He is your rock and your strength and your shield.

28 April

"The Lord is my shepherd; I shall not want. He maketh me to lie down in green pastures: he leadeth me beside the still waters" (Psalm 23:1-2, KJV).

Prayer Point

Have you ever seen a shepherd leading a flock of sheep? He directs the sheep to places where He knows the pasture is green and the sheep will enjoy the pasture. He also ensures that the sheep stay together and do not get lost.

Lord Jesus is our Good Shepherd who we should trust with our lives because He knows the best pastures for us. His aim is to lead us to the green ones to make sure that we stay in his ways and we don't get lost.

Allow the Good Shepherd to lead you. Don't lose focus until you land on the green pastures. The existing storms in your life will subside—and God will lead you through the still waters. Trust him; He is your Shepherd.

29 April

"Sow to yourselves in righteousness, reap in mercy; break up your fallow ground: for it is time to seek the Lord, till he come and rain righteousness upon you" (Hosea 10:12, KJV).

Now is the time for dedicating more time to the things of God and seeking God's face and understanding on things that are happening around us so that we can spiritually position ourselves in places where God wants us to be. When you seek the Lord, you ought to do so until the Lord comes and rains righteousness upon you.

As you seek the Lord, you seek Him with the faith that He will satisfy your needs and He will give you your heart's desire. The Word of God says you ought to start sowing on that vacant land within. You can sow by seeking the face of God who will answer you and provide you with righteousness and mercy upon your life.

It is not necessary for us as children of God to find ourselves in situations where we are punished if we could obtain mercy from the Lord and be forgiven and our punishment uplifted. In God, it is never too late to start sowing in righteousness for your own benefit so that you can start anticipating the rain of righteousness.

30 April

"But if from thence thou shalt seek the Lord thy God, thou shalt find him, if thou seek him with all thy heart and with all thy soul" (Deuteronomy 4:29, KJV).

After I graduated from tertiary, I stayed for some time without a job. What made this worse was that on my final year of studying, I did not apply for any junior positions. I wanted to start working soon after my graduation, but this made me stay unemployed for a couple of months.

I continued to be very loyal and bought the newspaper with job adverts every Wednesday morning. I would browse through the newspaper and apply for positions every morning, but I could not get a response or an interview.

One day, I decided to seek the Lord in prayer and fast for five days, from 6:00 in the evening until 6:00 the next evening. I prayed with so much faith since I had no doubt in my heart that God would answer me. I got my breakthrough on day three of my fast when I was called for an interview. I was so excited because God was so real. I just couldn't believe it! God has done similar things for so many people and He can do it for you. All it takes is seeking Him with all your heart and all your soul and He will draw near.

Chapter 5

Be Persistent in Your Prayers until You Get a Breakthrough

1 May

"The end of the world is coming soon. Therefore, be earnest and disciplined in your prayers" (1 Peter 4:7, NLT).

If you were to take a look at what is happening in the world today, you would agree that most people don't seem to be bothered by the fact that they will pass on one day. Surprisingly, when something gets mentioned on the television or in the media about the end of the world or any natural disasters that are predicted, suddenly people start to panic.

The truth of the matter is that it really does not matter what part of the world you live in to start noticing the signs that the end of world is near. As children of God, we shouldn't get worried when we see all the signs happening because the Word of God tells us to be serious in our prayers and be disciplined because we don't know when the hour is going to be for Christ to return.

Having discipline in prayer involves building a routine in your life where you always dedicate some of your time to prayer and fasting regardless of what is happening around you. Being disciplined means that—even when you have other commitments—when your time to pray comes, you simply excuse yourself and go into a private space where you talk to God. There are many benefits that we get from talking to God; one of those is to be protected from the things that can cause us to sin or protection for our family or those close to us.

God wants to hear from us always. When we remember him, He gets delighted. We have to bear in mind that prayer is not for God; it is for your benefit. Things of the world and the world itself will perish, but God and those who have been working to serve and obey Him will be saved.

Prayer of the Day

Dear God, help me to stay disciplined in my prayers unto you. Help me, Father, to allow your words to sink and remain in my mind, soul, and body. Teach me to use my time wisely so that I may not miss a fellowship with you. Grant me the drive to be disciplined in my prayer life that I may conquer until my time on earth comes to an end. In Jesus's name.

2 May

"If my people, who are called by my name, will humble themselves and pray and seek my face and turn from their wicked ways, then will I hear from heaven and will forgive their sin and will heal their land" (2 Chronicles 7:14, NIV).

Prayer Point

Imagine being in a situation where you know you were trapped into sin and you had a challenge because you did not know how to face God and ask for forgiveness. If you humble yourself and pray and seek God's face and are willing to repent of your sins, then He will hear you and forgive your sins and all will be well where you live.

Sometimes God does not respond to our prayers because we are separated from Him. A wall of sin is preventing God from showing interest in us and making things well for us. I invite you to pray against any element of pride or any form of sin that could be prevalent in your life at the moment and ask God to restore you.

There could be areas in your life where you have been walking in disobedience—or have been unfaithful. This is a great opportunity to confess your sins before God as you pray and turn away from unfaithfulness and become faithful and obedient to God so that the yoke of bondage can be removed. The Lord is faithful; He will forgive you. You just need to confess and repent whenever you approach the throne of grace.

3 May

"So what shall I do? I will pray with my spirit, but I will also pray with my mind; I will sing with my spirit, but I will also sing with my mind" (1 Corinthians 14:15, NIV).

Prayer Point

There are certain times in life when you just feel you have said all different types of prayers to God and you probably don't have words tell Him. In times such as those, when you pray, you need to consider the spirit. Praying in the spirit will enable your spirit to pray to God and the Holy Spirit will give you utterance (Acts 2:4).

Pray that God helps you to pray regularly as He so directs you. Ask God in prayer to fill your heart with the Holy Spirit so that you may never run out of prayer items—you may only look at every situation as an opportunity to draw closer to God.

Ask for wisdom from God—to lead you into regular praying and talking to God. Pray in the spirit often when you don't know what to pray for because your spirit knows what you ought to pray for.

4 May

"Is any one of you in trouble? He should pray. Is anyone happy? Let him sing songs of praise. Is any one of you sick? He should call the elders of the church to pray over him and anoint him with oil in the name of the Lord. And the prayer offered in faith will make the sick person well; the Lord will raise him up. If he has sinned, he will be forgiven. Therefore confess your sins to each other and pray for each other so that you may be healed. The prayer of a righteous man is powerful and effective" (James 5:13-16, NIV).

Prayer Point

There is no excuse not wanting to communicate with God regularly. In times of happiness, we should sing songs of praise; in times of trouble, we should call upon God to rescue us. When we are sick, we should call upon the name of the Lord to be healed; in financial crisis, we should pray to God to provide for us.

Pray that God reveals secrets behind your illnesses so that if the cause of your sickness is sin-related, you can confess your sins in order to be set free. Aim for righteousness in your Christian walk.

Ask God to lead and guide you into people you should pray with— people who even when you find it hard to pray you can ask on your behalf to pray for you. Pray for that relationship and the fellowship that you will have with the Christian brethren that you may grow as you continue to pray for each other.

5 May

"And pray in the Spirit on all occasions with all kinds of prayers and requests. With this in mind, be alert and always keep on praying for all the saints. Pray also for me, that whenever I open my mouth, words may be given me so that I will fearlessly make known the mystery of the gospel" (Ephesians 6:18-19, NIV).

Prayer Point

Whenever you pray, on all occasions, be alert about what is happening around you and in the spiritual realm. Staying in touch with God will make you stay in tune with what God is saying to you at that point.

Pastors and other servants of God serving you in your place of fellowship also need to be prayed for so that they can convey God's messages in the manner that is expected and so that they can clearly communicate the mysteries of the Kingdom to the church as God directs them.

Ask God to give you the ability to consider the spiritual needs of other believers so that when you pray, you can pray for them also.

6 May

"Answer me when I call, O God of my righteousness; Thou hast set me at large when I was in distress: Have mercy upon me, and hear my prayer" (Psalm 4:1, ASV).

Prayer Point

God always responds to all our prayers and the response can be yes, no, or later. God knows what is best for us and He never makes a mistake. You could be crying out to God to remove a certain discomfort in your life and you've been waiting for an answer. Don't give up. Press on and pray that He gives you the ability to persevere until you get an answer.

Pray for all things, believing that God will answer you. Believe that the situation that you face—no matter how difficult—shall pass.

Pray that your strength gets renewed so that you can be in a position to hear and receive from God. Avoid panicking and seeking shortcuts other than God because—even though they may seem to work for a while—they will cost in the long run.

7 May

"Love does not delight in evil but rejoices with the truth. It always protects, always trusts, always hopes, always perseveres" (1 Corinthians 13:6-7, NIV).

Prayer Point

A measure of love is not by how much we say we love; it is measured in terms of our actions. When we demonstrate actions that always protect and always trust in God and have hope in God—no matter the circumstances and having the heart to endure in hardships—we would be showing love.

Pray that God fills your heart with love that will be so powerful that it will command every part of your body to conform to God's standards. Pray that—in everything you do—you can be controlled by the loving emotion in you.

God did not create all people in the world with smiley faces to show that we are loving people. He knew that a smiley face was not a requirement to show love. It does not matter whether people see you as a loving person or not. The love that comes from God in your heart and your actions will bear testimony. God does not look at the outward appearance; He looks at the heart (1 Samuel 16:7).

8 May

"Devote yourselves to prayer with an alert mind and a thankful heart" (Colossians 4:2, NLT).

If you are devoted to something, you are likely to enjoy doing it. Your mind, body, and soul should be devoted to communication with God. Your mind should stay alert during prayer so that you can pray a relevant prayer to God and, most importantly, the prayer that is needed at that particular point in time. We tend to devote some of our time to do other things, but devoting some of our time to the things of God is much more essential. When our minds are alert, we pray for things that are relevant because the spirit in you will be sensitive and prompt you to things that are important.

Spiritual growth comes as a result of continuous prayer to God and having the desire of wanting to receive from God. When you feel heavy, prayer provides you with an opportunity to take off the load and be left to feel lighter.

It is also important to note that prayer is not always about complaints or never-ending requests; it is an opportunity for every believer to say thank you to God for all the good things that He keeps on doing for us—even the things we sometimes take for granted.

One day I asked my son to pray—he was only five years old—and it was our bedtime prayer. He said very few powerful words in that short prayer. He said, "Lord, thank you for such a beautiful sunny day. Amen." It was winter and God had decided to give us a sunny day that most people enjoyed. What got me thinking about my son's prayer is that if I had to pray that evening, my prayer would have been in a form of a request for protection, but my son felt the need to thank God during that devoted time.

Commitment to prayer is crucial to the survival of every Christian today. People need to be constantly praying in order to be given an understanding of the things of God and so that they can be rightly positioned. A prayerless life leads to many evil attacks because it makes a person vulnerable.

Prayer of the Day

Dear Heavenly Father, thank you for choosing me before I even knew myself. Thank you, Lord, for loving me as I am. I want to devote myself to be in constant meetings with you. Allow the Holy Spirit to guide me through all the conversations with you and to give me the ability to pray for things that matter to me and your kingdom. In Jesus's name I pray. Amen.

9 May

"Ye ask, and receive not, because ye ask amiss, that ye may consume it upon your lusts" (James 4:3, AKJV).

Prayer Point

A prayer that God answers is a prayer that is not based on selfish reasons or ambitions. It is a prayer that God sees other people as well getting blessed when it is answered. A prayer that is not based on a need but on what you want does not often win God's favour because what you want may not be what you need.

Pray that God helps you to have a heart that is full of humility and is considerate. Pray that God meets all your needs and that He reveals to you His will for your life in each and every situation.

Allow the power of the Holy Spirit to dwell within your spirit and provide guidance to you so that you are in a better position to pray the prayers that are in line with God's mind and heart so that you can start receiving.

10 May

"Be joyful always; pray continually; give thanks in all circumstances, for this is God's will for you in Christ Jesus" (1 Thessalonians 5:16–18, NIV).

Prayer Point

Joy comes from the Lord through the Holy Spirit. Joy is not a result of what happens to us from the outside; it is what happens to us from within. The Word of God today is urging you to give thanks in all circumstances; whether a circumstance is good or bad, we ought to thank God for it for it is the will of God for you.

It can be quite difficult to thank God when we have just recently lost a loved one and we are still in shock and going through a lot of pain. What we need to realise is that some things happen in order to take us one step up in terms of our faith in God and looking up to Him for our every need because what we have, our parents, relatives and kids came from Him.

Let it be your prayer to stay in constant fellowship with God and to have a heart that is full of joy in all circumstances. Pray that God grants you understanding in everything that happens in your life and thank God for all the circumstances and the lessons that come with them.

11 May

"If you, then, though you are evil, know how to give good gifts to your children, how much more will your Father in heaven give good gifts to those who ask Him!"(Matthew 7:11, NIV).

Prayer Point

Sometimes, in order for us to receive from God, we need to have a close relationship with God to such an extent that we know what to ask from to Him at a specific season of our lives. Prayer is a powerful weapon for us to use to request not only tangible things but for us to request the intangible gifts that God has in store for us so that we can start bearing fruit and expanding His Kingdom.

If you have never prayed to God for a specific gift or to grow in one of gifts that God has blessed you with, I urge you to ask God to give you one of the good gifts He has in store for you so that you can start experiencing God's greatness beyond what you have experienced.

Lastly, pray that God may use you for His Glory in the way that He deems fit. Also pray for other people that you know whom God has blessed with special gifts but are using those for wrong purposes. Pray for their conviction so that they can find their way to Lord Jesus Christ and may use the gifts for His glory.

12 May

"The Lord is far from the wicked but he hears the prayer of the righteous" (Proverbs 15:29, NIV).

Prayer Point

There are many things that can make a person live a life that has no meaning. Things such as indulging in things of the flesh like lust, alcohol, and drug abuse and many others that make people wicked. These things become a wall of hindrance between a person's prayers and God.

God wants every believer to live a righteous life for His ear is closer to the prayer of the righteous than the cries of the wicked. Pray that, by the grace of His power, God keeps you in a righteous standing with Him so that whenever you call on Him, He may answer you.

Pray to God to help you overcome any weaknesses you might have—addictions and all the bad habits—so that you may experience a prayer life full of answers from God. Pray that God directs you into talking, acting, and fellowshipping righteously.

13 May

"I want men everywhere to lift up holy hands in prayer, without anger or disputing" (1 Timothy 2:8, NIV).

Prayer Point

I have failed in many occasions to pray when I was not in control of my emotions or when I was angry. When you are unable to pray because you are angry, you are allowing the evil one to steal time to talk to God.

God is a peaceful God and in order for Him to receive your prayer, you must pray in peace, without anger or arguments. You must have forgiven everyone who has wronged you.

Ask God to help you deal with all the bitterness, anger, disappointment, and resentment in your heart—and that your heart may be lighter when you pray and only pray from a pure heart that is only focusing on godly matters. Ask God to help you forgive those who have wronged you as you stand in prayer today.

14 May

"The Lord detests the sacrifice of the wicked, but the prayer of the upright pleases Him" (Proverbs 15:8, NIV).

Prayer Point

God cannot be fooled by any man in the world because He knows what is in our hearts. God is not interested in the expensive gifts you can offer in church for other people to see. He is interested in the righteousness of your heart. The story of Cain and Abel shows us that God accepts the sacrifice of a righteous man like He did with Abel (Genesis 4:1-10).

You know your thoughts—how good or bad they are—and you know that God is pleased with a man whose thoughts and ways are righteous. Make it your prayer request that God removes any evil motive in your heart so that when you stand in prayer, your prayers can be accepted by God.

Seek righteousness in all your works so that you may bring delight to God when you pray. Pray that God can position you in a place that will make you more favoured in his sight. Reject evil desires and entertain righteous living.

15 May

"Do not be anxious about anything, but in everything, by prayer and petition, with thanksgiving, present your request to God" (Philippians 4:6, NIV).

When we are not sure of the outcome or we are worried about the future, we often get anxious. Anxiety is a biological process that makes us react differently with fear to things that are going to happen in the future. A student who awaits the final exam results could spend sleepless nights due to the anxiety because of not knowing whether he has passed the exams or not. Some people's anxiety makes them moody because they are full of fear of the outcome. At least once in a lifetime, we all get anxious because of a certain circumstance we are expecting in our lives. Lack of faith and fear of the outcome is the main cause of anxiety because when you are anxious, you are already living in the future with fear.

The scripture says "do not be anxious." That is a command that we must not even consider as an option and it clearly states that we must not be anxious about anything. Instead we must present or table all our worries to God. This simply tells us that all the things that we are often anxious about are not for us to solve but for God. When you are anxious, you are not solving. Your mind works very hard because it is processing the same information over and over and it makes you even more terrified.

The best way to deal with anxiety is to immediately convert all worries to prayer requests and pray to God to help us. Thanksgiving softens the heart of God because it affirms to God who is in our lives and how great and important He is in our lives.

For all the challenges that you come across in life, refuse to be overwhelmed by fear and anxiety. In prayer and fasting, surrender your concerns to God and wait to receive a breakthrough. When you present your requests to God through prayer and petition, you are saying to God that you surrender all your life for there is nothing compared to the price that Jesus paid on the cross. You are releasing your faith. God loves it when you show complete faith and confidence in Him. There is nothing bigger than Him and there will never be anything bigger or more powerful than God.

Prayer of the Day

Dear Heavenly Father, I know, at times, I live in the future and become anxious over things that are uncertain in my life. I come to you today, wanting to surrender all my problems and all the situations that are uncertain in my life. I dedicate every problem that is causing me to worry every day and I lay it on your table to solve. In Jesus's name. Amen.

16 May

"Seek the Lord while He may be found; call on Him while He is near" (Isaiah 55:6, NIV).

Prayer Point

There are many things that people seek in order to get fulfilled. Some pursue worldly riches because of wanting to earn respect, power, and happiness. Money and everything associated with it can bring happiness to a certain extent. Money can solve some of a person's problems, but when you seek God, you know that you have sought the right thing.

God does not want you to delay in calling Him. God wants you to call on Him while He is still near and get to enjoy His presence while He may be found. Seek God for revelation and spiritual elevation that is important for His kingdom.

Seek the Lord in prayer for all your needs—protection, health, business, success, and any area specific to your life. Seek God through his Word and sincere prayer.

17 May

"You have heard that it was said, 'Love your neighbour and hate your enemy.' But I tell you: 'Love your enemies and pray for those who persecute you'" (Matthew 5:43-44, NIV).

Prayer Point

The blood of Jesus brought unity and forgiveness of sins to every believer. The things that were not possible before Jesus came were made possible through Him. In Christ Jesus, no revenge is necessary when someone has wronged you.

Every person has enemies, but Jesus expects you not to hate your enemies. If you do, you will be promoting the evil behaviour of animosity.

Pray to God to help you retrieve all the people who have wronged you and release them in your heart. Ask the Helper, the Holy Spirit, to help you love those persons you know are your enemies and dedicate a prayer today for those people who persecute you.

18 May

"Let us then approach the throne of grace with confidence, so that we may receive mercy and find grace to help us in our time of need" (Hebrews 4:16, NIV).

Prayer Point

It is by grace that we found salvation through our Lord Jesus Christ. There are many people in the world who were born in countries where the gospel of Jesus Christ is not allowed to be publicly proclaimed. It is by God's grace that there are people who are able to pray to God in time of distress and any other time without hiding.

The mercy that we receive through Christ should make us even more humble because it is not by our own strength that we were saved. Through the grace of God and His mercy, Lord Jesus saved us.

Pray for the grace of God to multiply in all areas of your life. It is the grace of God you need to stay in good health and be prosperous. Pray for the grace of God to abound even to nonbelievers that they may recognise and appreciate the love of God in their lives.

19 May

"Ask and it will be given to you; seek and you will find; knock and the door will be opened to you. For everyone who asks, receives; he who seeks, finds; and to him who knocks, the door will be opened" (Matthew 7:7-8, NIV).

Prayer Point

A thought I used to have when I was young was that if God knows my thoughts, then He surely knows my needs. If He knows my needs, I should just receive from Him without much sweat. I believe most people have similar thoughts, but if we received what we needed from God automatically, there would be no communication with God. God wants us to communicate with Him so that there can be a reaction from His side.

Just as parents have kids to care for, they still expect their kids to ask for a new pair of shoes or toys because there is no relationship without communication. We ought to knock in order for the door to be opened and we ought to ask in order to receive because that is how we communicate our needs.

Ask God to meet all your needs. Ask in prayer everything that you need from God. Be specific about your needs. If you need a child, say it as it is; if it is a job, be specific regarding what you need and trust God to meet your needs.

20 May

"But when he asks, he must believe and not doubt, because he who doubts is like a wave of the sea, blown and tossed by the wind. That man should not think he will receive anything from the Lord" (James 1:7, NIV).

Prayer Point

You cannot doubt God if you believe that He is your everything in life. When you make God the centre of your life, you have no choice but to believe in Him for everything in your life. You won't omit God in anything because He would be your source.

God is pleased by someone who has complete faith in Him. Complete faith in God will stand the test of time. When you stand in prayer, believe that God will grant you the desires of your heart. God does not honour a faithless prayer.

Pray that God helps you in the knowledge of Him. Ask Him to guide you into ways of worship that will cement your faith in Him fully. Pray that God gives you the patience to wait for His answer as you put your request to God without wavering.

21 May

"If a man shuts his ears to the cry of the poor, he too will cry out and not be answered" (Proverbs 21:13, NIV).

Prayer Point

People have different needs. What some people consider to be the basics, others may consider a luxury. God expects us to care of the needs of others and assist wherever we can so that we can be in good standing with Him so that when we ask for something from God, He can answer us.

Every man on earth was created by God. God expects His children to show love to His creation by being God's eyes and hands to help the needy people in this world.

Pray that God helps you to meet the needs of the poor wherever possible and that you don't turn a blind eye to beggars on the street so that God can pay attention to your needs.

22 May

"Evening and morning, and at noon, I will pray and cry aloud; and He shall hear my voice" (Psalm 55:17, AKJV).

When I was young, I used to think that one only prays when there is a problem. As I grew older, I realised that one needs to pray about everything. God enjoys hearing from us—just as a father enjoys hearing from his children when they are away. God also enjoys hearing from us through prayer because it is a symbol of our faith in Him. When you dedicate your time to God, you are saying, "Lord, I know you are there for me and you care" and God likes that.

The psalmist persistently sought the face of God throughout the day. He knew that it's easy to fall into temptation without God in your life; he wanted to hear from God and speak to Him at least three times a day. How often do you talk to God in prayer in a day and do you think it's enough? It is important for us to talk to God as often as we can to reduce the chances of falling into temptation.

God wants you to persistently seek Him with all your Heart because that shows Him how serious you are about your relationship. A journey in my Christian walk revealed that God builds up your faith in Him. He may start by answering prayers instantly or within a short time. As we grow in faith, some of the answers only come after weeks, months, or years of serious prayer and fasting. He does this to test our level of faith in Him and to let us grow in our faith in Him. Don't get discouraged when you don't see the answer to your prayers; let it give you more reason to seek God's face. In due season, He will answer your prayers.

Prayer of the Day

Dear Father, grant me the strength to always seek you in spirit and in truth believing in my heart that you care for me. I ask for your wisdom and guidance to pray without ceasing until I receive my breakthroughs in all the problem areas in my life. Lord, you are a faithful God and I trust you with all my heart. Teach me how to seek you in different times of the day. In Jesus's name. Amen.

23 May

"Husbands, in the same way, be considerate as you live with your wives, and treat them with respect as the weaker partner and as heirs with you of the gracious gift of life, so that nothing will hinder your prayers" (1 Peter 3:7, NIV).

Prayer Point

A husband has a responsibility toward his wife. He is supposed to show respect and be considerate. When living in accordance with this scripture, you get to have your prayers answered; 1 Peter 3:1 shows the responsibility for wives to submit to their husbands.

Pray that God helps you to give due recognition that your family, spouse, friends, and colleagues deserve that nothing can hinder your prayers. Pray that God helps you to give compliments to your loved ones and to seek forgiveness when you've hurt someone so that nothing can stand in your way as you pray.

Pray for other people who you know have the same responsibility in their household, to love and respect their wives but are not doing so. Pray that this gets to their hearts so that nothing hinders their prayers.

24 May

"And as he taught them, he said, 'Is it not written: My house will be called a house of prayer for all nations? But you have made it a den of robbers'" (Mark 11:17).

Prayer Point

When Lord Jesus was on earth, He performed many miracles that we read about in the New Testament. Over and above this, He prayed for long periods and fasted. Lord Jesus was doing this for many reasons; one of those is for believers to follow in His footsteps and pray.

Churches today have various activities to make them attractive to nonbelievers and to make it exciting for the youth. The most important matter is for a church to remain a house of prayer.

Pray that God blesses the contribution that you make toward your church. Pray that everyone who visits your church gets touched by the manner of worship and that the visitors keep returning so they are moved by the strong presence of God in your church.

25 May

"Then Jesus told his disciples a parable to show them that they should always pray and not give up" (Luke 18:1, NIV).

Prayer Point

It is a good thing to be prayed for by the elders of your church or priests, but you need to get yourself empowered in order to pray for yourself. Jesus had an expectation of His disciples that they should pray persistently.

Allow the power of God to fill you with the desire of wanting to know more of God and what He wants you to do in His Kingdom. Seek to intercede for others and to pray that you can live a life that is pleasing to God and lacks nothing.

Pray without ceasing and do not give up. Allow God's power to help you to persevere in prayer—even when you see no breakthrough. The longer you pray, the more serious you prove your faith in God through Christ Jesus.

26 May

"One of those days, Jesus went out to a mountainside to pray, and spent the night praying to God" (Luke 6:12, NIV).

Prayer Point

Lord Jesus spent most of His time ministering, praying for the sick, and performing miracles. This was a very big responsibility because most of the time He had to give His time to be with other people in order to bless them. He often would withdraw from the crowds in order to pray for a very long time. Prayer was His way to recharge and to receive strength to face the challenges of this world and to overcome temptation.

Life is full of many demands that can make it difficult to set aside the time to pray. As Christians, we ought to do as Jesus did and set aside time for us to talk to God for as long as we can. We get to be refreshed and anointed so that we can be equipped with the power of God to face the challenges of this world.

Pray that God helps you overcome spiritual laziness so that you can make the time to pray. Even in the midst of a busy schedule, make the time to pray because the devil is always looking for someone to devour. Don't leave a gap—pray.

27 May

"Whatever you ask in my name, this I will do, that the Father may be glorified in the Son" (John 14:13, ESV).

Prayer Point

There is no name more powerful than Jesus. Through this name, doors that had long been closed are opened. Through this name, you get healed of sickness. Through His name, no weapon formed against you shall prosper.

If you have needs in your life, ask God to meet them through the powerful name of our Lord and Saviour Jesus Christ. Jesus has promised that whatever you ask in His name, He will do it.

Use the powerful name of Jesus Christ in prayer to seal all your requests unto the Father. Ask whatever you need in the name of Jesus and it shall be done; there is no name above the name of Jesus.

28 May

"This is the confidence we have in approaching God: that if we ask anything according to his will, He hears us. And if we know that he hears us—whatever we ask—we know that we have what we asked of Him" (1 John 5:14-15, NIV).

Prayer Point

God expects us to have complete faith in Him. The faith that is not formed of anything we can touch nor see is based on the knowledge and the belief in our Lord and Saviour Jesus Christ. When you pray believing to God that He hears you, whatever you ask will be granted—bearing in mind that it should not be a selfish prayer.

Pray for the revelation of how your prayer should be in order for it to be aligned to God's will. Pray more in the spirit so that God can unveil powerful thoughts that He planted in your spirit that will guide you through the right direction.

Ask God to grant you the wisdom to pray the prayers that will be answered so that Jesus can be glorified and He can bring glory to God.

29 May

"Then said Jesus to those Jews that believed on him, If ye continue in my word, then are ye my disciples indeed" (John 8:31, KJV).

Prayer Point

If you continue in His Word, then you are His disciples. You can only continue once you have started something. Jesus wants us to start a relationship with Him and continue in our knowledge of Him and His works.

Our life is a journey and Lord Jesus wants us to start on this journey and be able to persevere and continue in His Word so that we can become His disciples. His disciples are meant to continue His works and encourage other believers to do that.

What has your life been like since you met Christ and invited Him to become your Lord and Saviour? Have you been continuing in His word? Whatever answer you give, pray that the Holy Spirit grants you the ability to continue your journey in Christ and never quit.

30 May

"For the vision is yet for an appointed time, but at the end it shall speak, and not lie: though it tarry, wait for it; because it will surely come, it will not tarry" (Habakkuk 2:3, KJV).

Prayer Point

Have you been waiting on the promises of God in order for something to arrive in your life? You will be comforted to know that when God has promised to give you something, He will always do it at the appointed time. His time may not be the same time as what you had expected, but it will be the right time for you to receive it.

When God promises to give you something, it will be complete. God does not give something that is half-baked; everything good and perfect comes from God. God gives us good and perfect gifts at the appointed time so that when we finally receive it, it will bring glory to His name.

You could be waiting on a promise or a vision that God has once told you would come your way. As you wait for that promise to be fulfilled, meditate on this scripture until you are satisfied when it ultimately gets fulfilled. Wait upon the Lord for His promise to be fulfilled upon your life; it will never delay.

31 May

"Be still before the Lord and wait patiently for him; do not fret when men succeed in their ways, when they carry out their wicked schemes" (Psalms 37:7, NIV).

Prayer Point

As we go through life, we see some of our peers or brothers and sisters becoming more prosperous than we are and it often brings feeling of inadequacy. The Word of God is telling you to be still and wait patiently upon the Lord because God has not forgotten you.

Just as there are flowers in the world that blossom during different seasons, you are a unique flower that will start blossoming at the right season that is only known to God. Do not worry when you feel other people are succeeding and you are not because God has not forgotten about you.

Remember that what may seem like success on the outside could be the fruit of an evil activity that some people engage in. Since you don't know, you might envy their wealth and prosperity. Patiently wait upon the Lord to bless you with the blessings that come from heaven and pray in the meantime that God gives you the wisdom to take care of those future blessings.

Chapter 6

Be Hopeful for Things to Turn Out for Your Own Good

1 June

"Forget the former things; do not dwell on the past. See I am doing a new thing! Now it springs up; do you not perceive it? I am making a way in the desert and streams in the wasteland" (Isaiah 43:18-19, NIV).

When you are driving a car or riding a bicycle, it is often difficult or impossible to progress when your focus is on the things that you have driven past. One could make terrible accidents that could even cost lives. The same is true about life since life is a journey. We can only see what God is about to do in our lives if we pay attention to what God is about to do instead of dwelling on the bad experiences of the past.

It is important to remember that what is in the past cannot be changed; it remains in the past. If your past is full of pain and suffering—instead of praying and hoping for a better future, you constantly replay the video of the past memories—it could make you feel depressed. This scripture tells us to let go of the past; let go of yesterday's disappointments and look around to see the things that God is starting to do in your life.

God is making a way in the desert and streams in the wasteland for you. God wants you to be happy and all you need to do is to open your mind and heart and receive from God. One thing the enemy will try to do is to stir up your emotions by constantly reminding you of your past disappointments and failures. When you start having negative thoughts about your past, rebuke those thoughts and look up to God.

He always has a bright future for us. Your destiny is not over since you have a victorious life through Christ Jesus and "you can do all things through Christ Jesus who gives you strength" (Philippians 4:13). From today, focus on what is coming and not what has passed; you cannot change the past. God can change your future and make it even better for you. Remember that today will be tomorrow's past; make sure that you celebrate today and hope for a bright future.

Prayer of the Day

Dear Lord, I have been disappointed, lied to, hurt, and betrayed by different people in my life. Here I am today, surrendering my past hurts to you. I release everyone who has wronged me in my life. Whether the person has asked for forgiveness or not, I choose to forgive them all. I want to receive the great things that you have planned for me. Help me, Lord, to start a good chapter in my life from today. I receive all the good things that you have predestined for me. I refuse to be reminded of my terrible past; if any thought of the past creeps in my mind, let it be in the form of an inspiration. In Jesus's name I pray. Amen.

2 June

"May the God of hope fill you with all joy and peace in believing, so that by the power of the Holy Spirit you may abound in hope" (Romans 15:13, ESV).

Prayer Point

It is only God who can fill your heart up with hope because that hope is only through His Son Jesus Christ. When you look at things that are happening around the world today, it is scary. People lose their loved ones and there are many diseases that kill a lot of people. I don't know how those who don't have Jesus in their lives survive. For me, accepting Jesus was not an option but a must.

Let your focus this day be on looking up to Lord Jesus who is our only hope. In all areas where you need His guidance and His peace to fill you in, seek Him in prayer, believing that He is all that you need to face tomorrow.

Pray that God removes everything that is hindering your spiritual growth. Pray that whatever situation looked hopeless in your life, you start finding hope through Jesus Christ. If you thought it was over with your marriage, start hoping that God will restore your marriage. Allow God to fill your heart with joy and everlasting peace in your heart, in Jesus's name, so that you can continue to trust in Him in all circumstances.

3 June

"Be of good courage, And He shall strengthen your heart, all you who hope in the Lord" (Psalm 31:24, KJV).

Prayer Point

Sometimes one goes through so much emotional pain that, even if you had some of your best friends or family members tell you not to worry and say that things you will be all right, you would still not feel all right.

Refuse to be discouraged even in the most trying circumstances. Pray that the Holy Spirit may lift you up so that you may feel encouraged and remain strong as a soldier in Christ Jesus.

Ask Jesus to revive your spirit so that where there was hopelessness, you can find hope. Refuse to worry about things that concern the future; pray about them and trust God to see you through.

4 June

"'For I know the plans I have for you,'" declares the Lord, "'plans to prosper you and not to harm you, plans to give you hope and a future'" (Jeremiah 29:11, NIV).

Prayer Point

God is sovereign and He has your future and destiny in the palm of His hand. His plans for your future are only known to Him. In order for you to continue hoping for a great future, you need to start believing that God's plans will make you prosperous and not fail you. This does not mean that when you write an exam, you will always pass; it means that even when you achieve unexpected results, you must not stop trying. Even if it could look like a failure on the outside, God has dealt with your character and God has taught you perseverance. He wants you to value what you receive at the end because things that we easily get, we don't often value that much.

In situations where you find yourself surrounded by people who often pass condescending remarks in order to try to make you feel worthless, know that God has good plans for you—no matter what any person can say. God wants you to know and believe during this hour that what He told Jeremiah still applies to you. He is a God who honours his Word and He never changes or fails.

Tell God that you believe in the power of the resurrection of Lord Jesus and call to life every condition in your life that looks dormant in the name of Jesus that you may be strong and continue living a life of hope in Christ Jesus. Amen.

5 June

"But the needy will not always be forgotten, nor the hope of the afflicted ever perish" (Psalms 9:18, NIV).

Prayer Point

At a certain point in our lives, we all face some needy moments that are not for material things or wealth. It could be a need for a relationship, peace, or appreciation. As you read this message today, I want to encourage you that, whatever needs you may have, God has not forgotten you. You may feel inadequate in certain areas, but know that God has not forgotten about you.

As you pray today, remind God of the lack in your life and cling to your hope in Christ Jesus in anticipation of a relief that God will send your way. Pray for all the needy people that you know that God may remember them and bless them in due season.

Acknowledge that the pain you have endured in life has gone noticed in God's sight. Ask God to grant you a forgiving heart so that you may continue having faith, believing that God cares for all your emotional and physical needs.

6 June

"Let us hold fast the profession of our faith without wavering for He is faithful that promised (Hebrews 10:23, KJV).

Prayer Point

Our faith in God through Jesus Christ is the way we connect and a way in that we are able to receive the blessings, deliverance, and healing and all other good things from God. Through faith in Christ Jesus, we were saved. Through our continued faith in Him, we have learnt to rely and trust in Him on all the things. Faith in God through Christ Jesus requires firmness because God is always faithful.

Make it your prayer point that your faith in God continues to increase so that you can see the full manifestations of the blessings of God upon your life. Even if storms come your way, stand firm upon the promises of God.

Thank God for your life and that He knew you before you were born, He has your life clearly mapped out and He knows your destiny. Pray that God turns every negative circumstance in your life into a positive, any curse into a blessing, any defeat into victory, in Jesus's name. Amen.

7 June

"But Christ is faithful as a son over God's house. And we are His house, if we hold on to our courage and the hope of that we boast" (Hebrews 3:6, NIV).

Prayer Point

To stay in Christ requires a continuous application of our faith through the courage we demonstrate when things go differently. Our hope in our Lord Jesus is something that we should boast about for it is hope that leads to eternity.

Sometimes we go through ups and downs; when it happens, our faith and hope in Christ Jesus should remain firm. We should continue demonstrating our courage by looking at Jesus and admiring Him for

His faithfulness. It was not an easy decision to be nailed on the cross; an ordinary person could have given God an excuse at the last minute and said "I can't do it because it is too much pain." Jesus remained faithful throughout.

Pray that God helps you not lose your hope in Him. Let God erect the pillars of faith in your life that—no matter how big the storm—you can trust in Him and not be moved by the storm. Be the one who moves the storm.

8 June

"Jesus looked at them and said, 'With man this is impossible, but not with God; all things are possible with God'" (Mark 10:27).

Life on earth consists of good and the bad things. The challenge is not what to do when something good happens; it is what to do when things around us change for the worst. That is when we tend to start asking questions, wondering why God allowed this situation to happen.

When we become blessed and everything goes well in our lives, we don't wonder why God is blessing us too much because we feel entitled to all the good things. As a born-again child of God, it is important to note that when things get terrible, God is not limited by what we see. There is nothing too small for God that does not to get his attention and there is nothing too big for Him that He cannot solve. God is more powerful than what you've envisaged. He is the God of miracles and He performs more miracles when you think He can't.

If you believe that God is the God of doing the impossible, breakthroughs that looked impossible in your life will start being possible. Even if people look at you and think you are too poor and there is no hope for your provision, God will provide for you. God is the creator of heavens and earth and everything that is in it; there is nothing too hard for Him (Jeremiah 32:17).

You could be looking at yourself and thinking God cannot use you because you have physical limitations. Don't buy that lie because it comes right from the enemy. Don't give power to situations that will discourage you. Believe that nothing is impossible with God (Matthew 19:26). If you continue trusting God and reminding him how great He is, miracles will start happening.

Prayer of the Day

Dear Heavenly Father I thank you for your Word. I thank you that it is always alive in my heart. Dear Father, I believe that all things are possible through you. Perform all those miracles that you could not do due to my lack of faith. Let me testify of your loving kindness in Jesus' name. I believe that nothing is impossible with you. Amen.

9 June

"Against all hope, Abraham in hope believed and so became the father of many nations, just as it had been said to him, 'So shall your offspring be'" (Romans 4:18, NIV).

Prayer Point

Abraham was a faithful servant of God; he feared God and was obedient to God. When God requested Abraham to do something for Him, he never argued with God or asked countless questions. When God asked Abraham to make a burnt offering of his son, Isaac, Abraham did as instructed because he had hope in God and knew that God was his source of everything, including Isaac.

Pray that God helps you have your full hope in Him. He is the Alpha and Omega and He knew you before you even knew yourself. He knows where you come from and where you are going. Have hope in the Lord and obey Him; He is forever faithful.

Pray that God fulfils His promises in accordance with His Word in your life, just as He promised Abraham that he would be the father of many nations. Pray a prayer of faith, knowing that God will never fail you.

10 June

"For everything that was written in the past were written to teach us, so that through endurance and the encouragement of the Scriptures we might have hope" (Romans 15:4, NIV).

Prayer Point

God plans everything and always does things with a purpose. He knew that on this day, you and I would be alive somewhere needing to hear from Him. He put His Word for us through the scriptures in order to speak to us and our circumstances at any point in time. The Bible is inspired by God and it is the Word of God that aims to encourage us to persevere so that we may have hope in God.

In order to hear from God, you must be prepared to listen. Listening will be in the form of hearing God's Word that can come to us through different channels. It could be preaching through other servants of God or through the self-reading of scriptures.

Pray that the Holy Spirit aids you to read and understand the scriptures so that you can be encouraged every time you pray and every time you read God's word. Pray that God helps you to hear from Him whenever you read or listen to His Word so that you can always rise above your circumstances through Hope in Christ Jesus.

11 June

"Three things will last forever—faith, hope, and love—and the greatest of these is love" (1 Corinthians 13:13, NLT).

Prayer Point

When we are on earth, the things that tend to draw people's attention are things that are tangible and popular according to the worldly standards. Those things only carry value when we are on earth; the minute we cross over, everything physical is insignificant or has no value at all.

The good intangible things are hope, love, and faith. No physical value can be attached, but these things carry much weight in God's kingdom of eternity.

Pray that God may help you have complete faith in him and also that He may teach you to love even the unlovable people you come across. Pray that God resurrects hope in your life so that you remain hopeful even when it seems hopeless—and to give you peace of mind knowing that He is in control.

12 June

"God is not unjust; He will not forget your work and the love you have shown Him as you have helped His people and continue to help them. We want each of you to show this same diligence to the end, in order to make your hope sure" (Hebrews 6:10-11, NIV).

Prayer Point

There are many ways that we can show love to God our Father. It could be through talking to Him often, obeying His statutes, and living a righteous life. Another way of showing our love to God is by helping God's people until the end of our days on earth in order to make our hope definite in God.

As you pray today, ask God to give you the courage to work for Him in a way that will be pleasing to Him and to fill your heart with hope and compassion that you may be able to live your life for God through serving His people.

Ask God to grant you the ability to continue doing good works for His glory and to persevere in all circumstances. Pray that God gives you the courage to continue doing good works.

13 June

"I pray also that the eyes of your heart may be enlightened in order that you may know the hope to which He has called you, the riches of his glorious inheritance in the saints" (Ephesians 1:18, NIV).

Prayer Point

The enemy can be cunning and deceive the saints in certain circumstances into believing that a situation is hopeless. As a child of God, you must know that there is no situation that is hopeless for your hope is in Lord Jesus.

Allow God to enlighten your heart so that you may start to see the glorious riches that you have been called to through Christ Jesus. When times are hard, remind yourself of the fact that you are entitled to the great inheritance of the saints.

Pray for the enlightening of your spiritual eyes so that even when a situation looks bad, you don't feel as if that is the end. Always anticipate victory to be the end result after each battle that you fight through the help of God.

14 June

"As a prisoner for the Lord, then, I urge you to live a life worthy of the calling you have received. Be completely humble and gentle; be patient, bearing with one another in love. Make every effort to keep the unity of the Spirit through the bond of peace. There is one body and one Spirit—just as you were called to one hope when you were called—one Lord, one faith, one baptism" (Ephesians 4:1-5, NIV).

Prayer Point

We are encouraged to live a life that matches the calling that God has called us to when we received Lord Jesus as our personal saviour. Humility and gentleness can only manifest in our lives the moment we allow the Holy Spirit to transform us. Through the work of the Holy Spirit, we will be able to show patience and love through one hope that we all have in Christ Jesus.

Search your heart before you pray in order to identify the areas that you are struggling with such as pride, impatience, and hatred. Surrender to the Holy Spirit so that He can teach you how to be humble and patient in areas where you have been impatient.

Pray for guidance by the Holy Spirit to strive for peace. Pray that God helps you live a life that is pleasing to Him from now on—a fulfilling life full of love.

15 June

"Jesus said to her, 'I am the resurrection and the life. He who believes in me will live, even though he dies; and whoever lives and believes in me will never die. Do you believe this?'" (John 11:25-26, NIV).

There is no doubt about the fact that everyone will someday pass on. Physical death is inevitable. It is a process that is painful and difficult to get used to. The words to comfort us regarding how to deal with physical death is that if you are saved by the blood of Jesus, even if you die you will live.

In the scripture above, Martha was sad that her brother Lazarus had died. She said to Jesus that if He came earlier then Lazarus would not have died (John 11:21). Martha was a person who knew the scripture well; she knew that Lazarus would rise again. Martha could recite the verses, but she wanted Jesus to do something about the death of Lazarus. Jesus brought Lazarus back to life and demonstrated the power of God that has been vested upon Jesus.

Jesus was nailed on the cross for our salvation and He rose from the dead as a sign that death has no power over him. As a believer in Christ, you should not mourn the death of a loved one who had accepted Christ in the same fashion as nonbelievers; you ought to cry and mourn with an understanding that when someone dies believing in Christ Jesus, they will live even if they die.

Do you believe that Jesus Christ conquered death and He is the resurrection and the life and that whoever believes in Jesus will live even if he dies?

Prayer of the Day

Dear Heavenly Father, I thank you for giving me your words of perfect assurance that you are the resurrection and the life—anyone who believes in you will not perish even if he dies.

Thank you Lord for the sacrifice you made on the cross for my sins to be forgiven and that I may have eternal life. Help me continue standing strong in my faith. You are an awesome God and you are alive. In Jesus's name. Amen

16 June

"But in your hearts set apart Christ as Lord. Always be prepared to give an answer to everyone who asks you to give the reason for the hope that you have. But do this with gentleness and respect" (1 Peter 3:15, NIV).

Prayer Point

The way we live as followers of Christ must demonstrate our hope in Him. I have seen and met some strong servants of God; even when life changed drastically for them, they never lost faith and hope in Jesus Christ. God requires this attitude from us as well; even when nonbelievers get to know of our misfortunes, they remain amazed and inspired by our hope in Jesus Christ that will be demonstrated by how we respond to challenges.

We have a responsibility as believers to respond with gentleness and respect to anyone who has a question concerning our hope in the Lord. Make it your prayer request that God grants you the wisdom and courage to respond to anyone who asks you about your hope and your ever-increasing faith in Christ Jesus.

Pray to God to help you remain courageous in situations where you feel scared, anxious, doubtful, or broken-hearted that you may stay strong. Pray that God increases your strength as you continue hoping in Jesus Christ.

17 June

"Be joyful in hope, patient in affliction, faithful in prayer" (Romans 12:12, NIV).

Prayer Point

When things are not going well in life—or as we would expect them to—it's likely that we will start to feel sad or want to hide our pain from others. Sometimes life just becomes so full of storms that even when one goes away, another one comes through. It is difficult to have the patience to endure and continue praying. I just want to remind you that no matter how good a moment can be or bad a situation can be, it shall all pass.

If prayer has been an area that you have been struggling with, ask God to teach you how to pray; prayer is a powerful weapon in times of affliction and pain. If you have been impatient or made decisions that were based on emotions, ask God to give you an enduring heart when afflicted.

Pray that the Holy Spirit may help you to pray more fervently and be filled with joyful hope. Pray for perseverance so that you may get through life's challenges and remain faithful regardless of circumstances. Expect the joy of the Lord to occupy your entire being as you spend more time in God's presence in prayer.

18 June

"We continually remember before our God and Father your work produced by faith, your labour prompted by love, and your endurance inspired by hope in our Lord Jesus Christ" (1 Thessalonians 1:3, NIV).

Prayer Point

God is pleased with His children when they master the way they should conduct themselves. God expects that we work through our faith that we have in Him and also do it with the love that we have in our hearts. Endurance is brought by the hope in Jesus Christ.

Ask God to give you the ability to endure suffering through the hope that you have in Christ Jesus and by remembering what Christ died for.

No matter how dark a situation is, surrender all your problems to God and trust in Him fully. Know that when you labour in love, endure in hope, and work in faith, God is pleased with you and will not turn a deaf ear on you.

19 June

"But since we belong to the day, let us be self-controlled, putting on faith and love as a breastplate, and the hope of salvation as a helmet" (1 Thessalonians 5:8, NIV).

Prayer Point

Lack of self-control leads to sin. In every area of our lives, we need to have self-control in order to focus and channel our efforts to where they are needed most. As Christians, we are at spiritual warfare where we need to have faith in God in order to be able to conquer. It is through our faith, love, and self-control that we are able to submit to God's authority in order for Him to step in our circumstances and help us overcome.

Pray that God helps you use your gift of salvation and your faith, love, and hope in Him to overcome the actions of the enemy and his disruptions. Pray that your faith remains in Jesus Christ for as long as you remain alive.

Pray to God to help you increase your love to people you are not related to, neighbours, and complete strangers where possible that He may work through you. Pray for self-control in all areas of your life and thank Him for the salvation through Christ Jesus.

20 June

"O Lord, you alone are my hope. I've trusted you, O Lord, from childhood" (Psalm 71:5, NLT).

Prayer Point

The psalmist had the privilege of knowing God from childhood and trusted him ever since. He witnessed all the wonders and mercies of the Lord and he got to believe that in everything that he had seen and experienced in life. God is his only hope.

I would like to encourage you this season that it does not matter what time in your life you started trusting in God, God has always been there because He created you. The devil may have stolen a lot of time from you and lied to you about where you should put your hope. He may have deceived you to put your hope in idols or other things that were not worth putting your hope to. Rejoice that you have found true hope in Christ Jesus.

Pray that your trust in God remains solid—no matter what you encounter in life. You may lose many things in life—family, friends and other personal possessions—but never lose your hope in God through Christ Jesus.

21 June

"But blessed is the man who trusts in the Lord, whose confidence is in him" (Jeremiah 17:7, NIV).

Prayer Point

It is common for a young person to think that he or she will stay young, but it does not work that way. When we are young and able, it is easy to trust in your own strength that you can run and win a marathon, but when you become of age, you tend to realise that you don't have the strength to do most of the things that you used to do. Beloved, you don't have to wait until you are old to start trusting in God because—even when you are young—you cannot do anything without God enabling you.

Long to be called the blessed one by living a life of humility that will demonstrate your trust and confidence in God. Thank God for every opportunity and ability. It is through the mercies of God that you are alive today; it does not matter whether you are young or old, you are alive because of the mercies of God.

Pray that God helps you trust in Him always because there is no one more powerful. He is not limited by age or ability; He is the creator of the entire universe. Pray for complete trust in Him that you may be blessed.

22 June

"Consecrate yourselves, for tomorrow the Lord will do amazing things among you" (Joshua 3:5, NIV).

We often engage in activities that can hinder God from doing amazing things in our lives. We often engage in gossip, are ungrateful of so many things, or complain a lot. We need to set aside time in our lives and wait for God to do amazing things. When you set aside time to be with God, things that are happening around you will not matter.

Beloved, I want you to be reminded today that making our thoughts unclean and dwelling in things that are not godly will delay God from doing amazing things in our lives; we are delaying our own blessings. God's hand is full of blessings that are meant to land on His children. However, unless we dedicate ourselves, the amazing things that God has planned to bless us with shall not come.

I met a lady who could not have children for years. Only after she had made a decision to start a ministry that looked after the needs of abused women did God open her womb. She conceived naturally when she decided to make God's things a priority.

My prayer for you is for you to set aside special time of holiness and wait for God to do that amazing thing you have been waiting for. Look up to God and submit yourself to His authority and He will do amazing things in your life.

It is important that we keep our minds and hearts focused upon Jesus. Even when unexpected disruptions come our way, we must look up because we are reminding God that we have complete faith in Him that He will turn things around for us. Strive for holiness so that you do not miss the amazing things that God has predestined for us.

Prayer of the Day

Dear Heavenly Father, I thank you for reminding me always of what is required of me as your child. I recommit my heart to you and allow you to cleanse it and make it pure. I reclaim all the amazing things that were put on hold because I was not patiently waiting. I reclaim all the blessings that the enemy has stolen from me. Occupy every room in my heart, in Jesus's name. Amen.

23 June

"But the eyes of the Lord are on those who fear him, on those whose hope is in his unfailing love" (Psalms 33:18, NIV).

Prayer Point

The Bible is full of examples of servants of God who feared God; Abraham, Noah, and Enoch were God-fearing men. They loved God and obeyed his commands and God remained faithful in their lives. It is so comforting to know that the eyes of the Lord are on those who fear Him and whose hope is on His unfailing love.

Beloved, make Christ in your life a reality so that you can live in a way that shows obedience and fear of the Lord where you can live joyfully knowing that God is in control and fully watching over you.

Pray that your hope in eternity through Christ Jesus may increase. Pray for the wisdom through the Holy Spirit to renew your mind and your growth in doing the things that will be pleasing to God.

24 June

"For what was glorious has no glory now in comparison with the surpassing glory. And if what was fading away came with glory, how much greater is the glory of that that lasts! Therefore, since we have such a hope, we are bold" (2 Corinthians 3:10-12, NIV).

Prayer Point

The hope that has been given to us by the sacrifice that was made through Jesus Christ is sufficient to encourage us to remain strong in faith for there is nothing compared to our hope in Jesus Christ.

Our hope in Lord Jesus will remain because it is everlasting hope. Jesus was raised from the dead. Jesus remains our hope even beyond physical death for we are able to witness His power that has defeated death itself.

Pray that God reveals to you the areas that you have not been showing the fear and respect that God deserves. Repent of your sins and trust in the Holy Spirit to assist you in living a God-fearing life.

25 June

"For you have been my hope, O Sovereign Lord, my confidence since my youth" (Psalms 71:5, NIV).

Prayer Point

It is a blessing to have young people enjoy their youth in the confidence and knowledge of God and learn to trust in Him from the early stage and grow in their knowledge of Christ. Pray that God gives you the wisdom to share the joys of having hope in Him as a young person—like David did—and ask God to help you to win souls to the Kingdom of God who will worship and praise Him from early stage.

Pray that God uses you as a vessel to attract young people to come to Christ and give their lives to Him that they may start living a life that is full of hope in God. Lack of hope in God in a young person can be destructive; when faced with setback, young people get depressed and some resort to substance abuse or suicide.

Pray for all the young people all over the world that God can touch their lives so that they can start knowing God and can start putting their confidence in Him.

26 June

"Now faith is being sure of what we hope for and certain of what we do not see" (Hebrews 11:1, NIV).

Prayer Point

Having faith is about believing that something will happen—and not having a clue regarding how it will happen—but being certain of the result. Faith requires action because, without action, it is dead.

A certain group of people who went to pray that it should rain the next day, but the next day, only one child came to the church with an umbrella.

Faith requires action from our side. When we pray for something trusting God for a breakthrough, our actions thereafter will tell if we are waiting upon the Lord or not. Pray for your faith in God to increase so that even when you see no sign of breakthrough, you know that God is at work and still in control. Pray that the Holy Spirit may teach you how to act and wait in faith.

27 June

"Praise be to the God and Father of our Lord Jesus Christ! In his great mercy He has given us new birth into a living hope through the resurrection of Jesus Christ from the dead" (1 Peter 1:3, NIV).

Prayer Point

God has been so merciful to us by the sacrifice He made of His own Son Jesus who died on the cross in order for us to be saved through our faith. There could be many areas in your life that are not showing signs of life because you have neglected your hope in Christ Jesus. Arise into the new hope that has been given to you through Christ Jesus and call to life everything that seems dead or dormant in your life and enjoy these benefits through Christ Jesus.

Pray for the spirit of revival that will show your full inheritance in Christ Jesus that you must never neglect. Reclaim your hope in Christ Jesus.

Pray a prayer that will help you identify areas where you lack the ability but are interested in so that you can serve in the body of Christ. Pray for the resurrecting power of Jesus to give you the ability to serve as your heart desires for His glory in Christ Jesus. Amen.

28 June

"For the grace of God that brings salvation has appeared to all men. It teaches us to say no to ungodliness and worldly passions, and to live self-controlled, upright, and godly lives in this present age. We wait for the blessed hope—the glorious appearing of our great God and Saviour, Jesus Christ, who gave himself for us to redeem us from all wickedness and to purify for himself a people that are his own—eager to do what is good" (Titus 2:11-14, NIV).

Prayer Point

It is by grace that we are saved. As we grow in Christ, this grace teaches us to say no to the ungodly things of this world and all the worldly passions that may look good on the outside but have been designed to destroy us at the end. As a child of God, we can only bear good fruit if we are led and guided by the Holy Spirit.

Pray that the spirit of God works in you so that you can desire the things that are godly and to also help you overcome all the worldly passions that are making you vulnerable to the enemy's attacks.

Pray for other saints who are battling to let go of worldly passions and have fallen from the ways of God due to lack of self-control that God may restore them and have them passionate about the things of Lord Jesus again.

29 June

"Now our Lord Jesus Christ himself, and God, even our Father, that hath loved us, and hath given us everlasting consolation and good hope through grace" (2 Thessalonians 2:16, KJV).

Prayer Point

We come from different family backgrounds and different cultural influences. Some have been fortunate enough to be born from families that honoured God for generations. No matter what challenges they encounter, they never lose their focus in God because they know that their hope is in God through the grace found in Christ.

God's love is enough to get us through every challenge that we come across in our lives. It is so powerful that it can overpower the memories of a bad upbringing.

The enemy does not want you to have peace in anything you do. He does not want you to have a future. When you are down, he wants you to stay down so that you can ultimately give up on life. God wants the best for you because He loves you so much. He wants to give you what even a good family background would not do for you. He wants to see you have hope in hopeless situations. Pray and cling to the hope that has been given to you through Jesus Christ.

30 June

"To them God has chosen to make known among the gentiles the glorious riches of this mystery, that is Christ in you, the hope of glory" (Colossians 1:27, NIV).

Prayer Point

When Adam disobeyed God, God was disappointed and hurt. He had to punish Adam and Eve in the form of curses that took over their blessings. Out of His love, He saw the need to have our sins forgiven if we made the right choices in life and accepted Lord Jesus as our Saviour. God gave us a chance to reclaim what the enemy made us to forfeit in the Garden of Eden.

God is full of mercy; even when we had wronged Him in a big way, He still found it within His heart to be merciful and sacrifice His Son's life for us. Our hope was brought back through Jesus and His resurrection from the dead.

Your life may look dim, but it will always be bright through Jesus Christ. For as long as you still take every breath with your heart looking up to Jesus for hope in all the areas of your life, relationships, and breakthroughs where you have not been prospering, God will come your way and lift you up.

Chapter 7

Ask for Wisdom
and Live a Fruitful Life

1 July

"If you need wisdom, ask our generous God, and He will give it to you. He will not rebuke you for asking" (James 1:5, NLT)

In order to manage any aspect of your life, a certain level of wisdom is needed to prosper. Wisdom is needed to choose the right career path—and to choose the right people to employ. Without wisdom from God, it's easy to fall into a trap of making wrong choices and end up in trouble. Lack of wisdom in life often leads to temptation that ultimately leads to sin.

When you ask God to bless you with wealth, ask God for the wisdom to use the wealth. If you are a married couple, God can choose to bless a woman and not the man with the ability to provide for her family financially. Since money gives power, wisdom is needed by the woman not to use the money to undermine or disrespect the husband because he is still the head of the family (Ephesians 5:23). The same goes for a rich man; wisdom is needed to stay humble and to appropriately demonstrate the God-given power and to continue loving your wife.

I always wondered what I would have asked for in the times of King Solomon if God approached me wanting to know my heart's desires. When you ask for wisdom, you have in essence asked for the spirit of wisdom that is the Holy Spirit who gives you guidance, insights, and revelations into all the things. Exodus 31:3 says, "I have filled him with the Spirit of God, giving him great wisdom, ability, and expertise in all kinds of crafts." As you enter a new season, I urge you to ask God to grant you wisdom like King Solomon who valued wisdom above all the worldly treasures.

We need wisdom to choose our battles in life, to study effectively, to make right choices, to prioritize the things that matter, and to avoid unnecessary mistakes. We need wisdom to raise kids, to be great husbands and wives, to hear God's voice, and choose the best paths. James 1:5 reminds us that if we lack wisdom, we should ask God, who gives generously to all without finding fault.

Prayer of the Day

Dear Father, I come before you knowing that without your Holy Spirit in me, I am nothing. I humbly ask you to grant me wisdom and understanding in all areas of my life. I want my spiritual eyes to be open in order to make better decisions and have the right priorities that will bring glory to your name. I receive your wisdom in Jesus's name. Amen.

2 July

"But the wisdom from above is first of all pure. It is also peace loving, gentle at all times, and willing to yield to others. It is full of mercy and good deeds. It shows no favouritism and is always sincere (James 3:17, NLT).

Prayer Point

Wisdom from God is pure. When you are filled with the wisdom, you are filled with the Holy Spirit and will be able to demonstrate the fruits of the spirit that are love and gentleness. The other important thing is that wisdom from God makes one humble.

Once you have received the gift of wisdom from God, it will be clear because you will be covered with humility and love. You will extend yourself to assist others in need and you will be compassionate and full of mercy. We ought to be merciful just as our father is merciful (Luke 6:36).

Pray that God grants you the spirit of wisdom that will guide you into making right decisions and choices that will bring glory to His

Kingdom. Apply the wisdom that God gives you to bless others and to be sincere.

3 July

"For jealousy and selfishness are not God's kind of wisdom. Such things are earthly, unspiritual, and demonic" (James 3:15, NLT).

Prayer Point

Have you ever felt jealous of a fellow Christian such that you felt their blessing should have come to you and not them? Jealousy is something that even children get to have without having been taught about it. It is just a feeling of insecurity that they possess—especially when they see their parents holding another child and they start crying, seeking attention.

No matter the roots of jealousy and selfishness in our lives, God does not approve of such behaviour because God wants us to know that He created each of us uniquely. Our gifts will be unique and also the seasons that we receive our blessings will be unique. Whenever we find ourselves being jealous of others, we need to rebuke that spirit of jealousy and ask for wisdom that will make us remain positively inspired through the success of others.

God's wisdom can bring the best out in you by inspiring you to be the best person whom God has created to do great things. Look to God for wisdom to handle the different types of circumstances and also grow in your understanding and knowledge of God.

4 July

"If you are wise and understand God's ways, prove it by living an honourable life, doing good works with the humility that comes through wisdom" (James 3:13, NLT).

Prayer Point

In our Christian walk, we start off as infants in our faith, but we grow with time and mature spiritually. It is with maturity that we begin to understand some of God's ways and start applying them in our lives and consequently live a respectable life.

God expects us to live a life that is respectable and humble and focuses on good works through God's wisdom. God is interested in a person's heart and the way we conduct ourselves in His kingdom.

It can be challenging to live a life of humility if your heart does not draw from God's wisdom. Pray that God helps you live a life that glorifies Him—a life of humility, generosity, and peace. A life that inspires other people to live a godly life.

5 July

"Let the Word of Christ dwell in you richly, teaching and admonishing one another in all wisdom, singing psalms and hymns and spiritual songs, with thankfulness in your hearts to God" (Colossians 3:16, ESV).

Prayer Point

When the Word of God dwells in you richly, it is inside of you in so much abundance. When you are full of God's Word, you think and speak the Word and your actions are likely to be influenced by God's word.

Allow the Word of God to dwell in you in abundance by reading, listening, and meditating on it so that you can teach and reprimand others when they go astray through God's word. The Word of God is so full of wisdom that when our carnal minds run out of ideas or solutions to the problems, the Word of God has a solution to our problems.

Get into the habit of reading God's Word daily and meditating upon it so that you can share the wisdom that you get through reading the scriptures. Prepare yourself to be available to guide other people through the scripture by the wisdom granted to you by the Holy Spirit.

6 July

"And we are instructed to turn from godless living and sinful pleasures. We should live in this evil world with wisdom, righteousness, and devotion to God" (Titus 2:12, NLT).

Prayer Point

The world that we live in has become so evil and some of the laws that have been passed promote wrongdoing. There is so much sin that is advertised in magazines and television. If a person does not have God in their lives, they basically live and are guided by this lawless society.

Scripture says that we ought to live in this evil world with wisdom because wisdom will enable us to discern what is right and what is wrong. Wisdom will tell us whether we are doing God's will with our actions. Wisdom from God will remind us of our responsibilities as Christians and will guide us into making the right decisions and praying the right prayers at the right time.

Pray for God to guide you into wisdom when surrounded by ungodly people so that ultimately with your God-given wisdom, you may convince people to turn their lives to God. Pray that you apply God's wisdom to deal with difficult employers, spouses, children, and other family members.

7 July

"You have been taught the Holy Scriptures from childhood, and they have given you the wisdom to receive the salvation that comes by trusting in Christ Jesus" (2 Timothy 3:15, NLT).

Prayer Point

It is every believer's responsibility to live a life that promotes godliness and draws other people to God. God has given us the gift of salvation because He knew that we would need it during our journey on earth. There could be other people younger than you that you can share the good news of the Holy Scriptures with and God wants to use what you have been taught to share with others so that they can be saved.

Let the wisdom that has been given by the Holy Spirit manifest as you share the good news of the gospel with others. Pray that God gives you the courage to share the good news to others so that they can give their lives to Jesus and start trusting Him as their saviour.

Let the Word of God come alive in you—that the wisdom intended by the scriptures may be revived and you may start bearing fruit.

Continue to pray that you touch the lives of people you interact with so that they may see the light of God through you.

8 July

"Teach us to number our days aright that we may gain a heart of wisdom" (Psalm 90:12, NIV).

Every person on earth has an expiration date that is known only by God. God determines when a person is born and when a person will die. The mistake we often make is to live a life as if our stay on earth is permanent. If we could always remember to ask God to teach us to number our days, we would dedicate some of our time to doing the things that have eternal significance. The enemy will always try to divert our thinking and priorities to the things that don't matter so that at the end of our days there is nothing to write to God about.

It takes God's wisdom to live a life with good priorities, knowing that our dying date is a secret; it could be few seconds from now or few months or years away. The heart of wisdom will always remind you of that limited time you have on earth and how to make use of that time for God's glory.

I attended a funeral ceremony for an old lady. Her child had just finished building a beautiful house for her, but it still needed to be painted. It was touching to note that at the time the paint was bought, she had requested that the paint be used to paint the church instead of painting her house. Little did she know that few weeks later she would die and would have done something good for the Lord. This lady had numbered her days and had a heart of wisdom that directed her to give to God close to her passing.

There could be certain areas in your life that you are not happy with and you are struggling to break loose from them. You need to ask for God's wisdom to fill your heart and make you aware of the fact that your days are numbered. The enemy will try to blind you and entice to continue sinning by whispering to you that you are still young and you can always give up your sin when you are old. Don't buy it because that is a lie. Your days are numbered, aim to live righteously and do God's will because you don't know your last date on earth. How we end our journey on earth determines our eternal destiny.

Prayer of the Day

Dear Lord, thank you for reminding me to number my days. Please help me get rid of all the sin in my life and live just for you. I want to be like the psalmist, Lord. Teach me to number my days correctly that I may gain a heart of wisdom and start living a life that is fulfilling to you. In Jesus's name. Amen.

9 July

"So we tell others about Christ, warning everyone and teaching everyone with all the wisdom God has given us. We want to present them to God, perfect in their relationship to Christ" (Colossians 1:28, NLT).

Prayer Point

In order for us to do a perfect job of winning unbelievers to Christ, we need to have God's wisdom. God's wisdom is sufficient to equip us with the approach we ought to use to speak to other people about Christ and His love for us. Sometimes knowing the Word of God without the wisdom that guides us into understanding may not be sufficient to get us to properly share the good news of the Gospel.

Pray for the wisdom of God to supersede your thinking whenever you share the good news about Christ to anyone. It is only when Christ's wisdom takes over our thinking that we see things the way He sees them and we may convey a message that directly comes from Him.

Ask God's wisdom to come before your words as you share the good news of the gospel to the people that you will meet in different areas of your life.

10 July

"God has united you with Christ Jesus. For our benefit, God made him to be wisdom itself. Christ made us right with God; he made us pure and holy, and he freed us from sin" (1 Corinthians 1:30, NLT).

Prayer Point

God is the ultimate source of all wisdom. It was through His wisdom that He created heaven and earth and everything that is in the world today. When Adam and Eve disobeyed Him, all mankind was under the curse because of the sin they committed.

It is by God's wisdom that He saw the need to redeem us from the sin that was caused by Adam and brought Jesus to die for our sins so that we could be saved from eternal death. Christ made us right with God because we are a new creation through Him.

Begin relying on Christ for all the wisdom you need to accomplish different things in life. Pray sincerely that you receive this wisdom to operate at a level of deep understanding and peace. Jesus bought you with a price that He paid at the cross; pray that the Holy Spirit helps you stay free from sin.

11 July

"Wisdom is a shelter as money is a shelter, but the advantage of knowledge is this: that wisdom preserves the life of its possessor" (Ecclesiastes 7:12, NIV).

Prayer Point

A shelter is a place of safety where you hide away when you need protection and rest. Wisdom is likened to money because when you have money, you can afford to make or buy yourself a shelter. Wisdom goes beyond being able to acquire a shelter because sometimes having a shelter does not mean that you will be protected. Wisdom will let you consider various alternatives into making a choice but end up making the best choice.

Wisdom is knowledge that is able to preserve the life of its possessor. When you have wisdom from God, you will not be concerned about how you will look after yourself or your needs; you will have the wisdom to know how to approach the throne of your provider with such requests.

You could have regarded material possessions as surety for shelter, but God is saying that He is the provider of everything. All you have to do is to ask for God's wisdom to fill you and protect you.

12 July

"So we have not stopped praying for you since we first heard about you. We ask God to give you complete knowledge of his will and to give you spiritual wisdom and understanding" (Colossians 1:9, NLT).

Prayer Point

At a certain point in our lives, we come to want to know what God's will for our lives is. Many people come to a certain point in their lives where they just want to know God's will for their lives.

God's will cannot be determined by asking a friend or a family member, but it is something that can be asked of God himself. He created you and He has the original plan for your life. He has His way of revealing His will for your life; it may be in the form of a dream or through your growing interest on the things that you do.

Pray for every person, saved or not saved, that God's will be revealed in that person's life that they may live a life of spiritual wisdom and understanding through Christ Jesus. Pray for God's will for your life to be revealed so that you can continue serving God the way He expects you to.

13 July

"The whole world sought audience with Solomon to hear the wisdom God had put in his heart" (1 Kings 10:24, NIV).

Prayer Point

Wisdom that comes from God cannot be bought by material possessions, but you can receive it by faith through prayer and requests unto God. When people heard about the wisdom of King Solomon, they were impressed because they knew it was unique and came directly from God.

The moment people start to see that you have the gift of wisdom in you, they will come to you to be prayed for, for counselling, and for guidance. Wisdom will draw people your way so that you can lead them into the right path through your words that will make a difference in their lives.

Pray for God's wisdom to fill your mind that you can have the ability to lead and make decisions as King Solomon did. Pray that God may use you mightily to share His Word and to be there for other saints in prayer.

14 July

"Choose some well-respected men from each tribe who are known for their wisdom and understanding, and I will appoint them as your leaders" (Deuteronomy 1:13, NLT).

Prayer Point

Moses became tired of being the one who had to be responsible for solving the problems that happened amongst the tribes (Deuteronomy 1:12). He had to request that the people choose some well-respected people to come forth so that they could be appointed leaders of the tribe.

In order to be recognised as someone who is suitable for leadership, there is a lot of wisdom that one needs to demonstrate. Moses in this verse wanted to appoint a suitable leader who would lead with wisdom.

Pray for the right wisdom that will make you legible to lead accordingly in different areas of your life.

15 July

"Joyful is the person who finds wisdom, the one who gains understanding. For wisdom is more profitable than silver, and her wages are better than gold" (Proverbs 3:13-14, NLT).

When you see other Christians who have had the most terrible things happen to them but despite they remain joyful, we often wonder how that came about. Wisdom coupled with understanding is what a person who is grief-stricken needs in order to easily recover from that state of depression and to live a normal life. Without wisdom and understanding, one can find it difficult to move forward. Even when you lose your father, mother, or child, the way you will mourn will not be same as when God has given you the wisdom to understand and allow you to mourn with understanding. There is a big difference between mourning with understanding and mourning without understanding where the latter can take long to happen.

Wisdom is more beneficial in life because it makes you effective when making decisions and choices. If you have a life that is filled with wisdom, you will always rise above any challenge that is set forth before you because God will reveal to you why you have to go through certain things. It is lack of wisdom that makes people jealous of others who may seem to be prospering in their lives, but it is with wisdom that one comes to understand that we all experience blessing in different seasons of our lives. All you have to do is rejoice with people who are having the best of their season at the same time, believing and trusting in God that your season will come where you will reap your harvest.

If there is one thing you should desire to have this season, desire wisdom to be one of the things that God should bless you with so that you can start moving forward and making progress.

Prayer of the Day

Dear Lord, I desire to be led by your wisdom in all the situations in my life. Grant me the spirit of wisdom just as you granted King Solomon who ruled with so much wisdom during his times. Grant me the spirit of wisdom as you gave Joshua after the death of Moses so that I may prosper in all aspects of my life. I know that without your spirit of wisdom, I lack knowledge and understanding. In Jesus's name. Amen.

16 July

"Don't be impressed with your own wisdom. Instead, fear the Lord and turn away from evil" (Proverbs 3:7, NLT).

Prayer Point

When you start noticing that you are more talented in certain areas than other people are or you are smarter in other subjects than most of your friends, it's easy to overlook the source of your wisdom. We need to be cautious and not become proud; continue fearing God for He is the source of all wisdom.

The Lord is the source of our life, joy, and strength. In everything that we have in life, we ought to thank Him for His precious gifts. We must have the fear of the Lord that will make us run to Him to give Him praise when we see Him enabling us to do the things that we could not do before.

In areas where you excel because of the God-given wisdom, thank God for that blessing; it is not your wisdom, but God's. Pray that you don't become proud—no matter how highly favoured you are, continue to live in fear of God and shun the evil.

17 July

"There the child grew up healthy and strong. He was filled with wisdom, and God's favour was on him" (Luke 2:40, NLT).

Prayer Point

When you read the new statement and read about Lord Jesus and consider the teachings and miracles that He performed during His time on earth, it is clear that He was so full of wisdom and was mightily used by God. Sometimes His disciples would ask Him questions and He would answer them using a parable that would not give them an obvious answer because He wanted His disciples to think and apply some wisdom in order to understand the parables.

You could have been praying that God helps you and your husband work things out so that your marriage could start becoming exciting. It is not always about asking God to turn things around for your good; it could be that you need to apply wisdom into your marriage to understand your spouse better so that you can improve on your weaknesses and work effectively to make it the happy marriage that God intended it to be.

As you dedicate your time to pray today, pray that your children live a life full of God's wisdom just like Jesus and that God's favour may be upon them for all the days of their lives. As you pray for your career, family, and church, pray that God gives you the ability to use wisdom to bring the best out of any situation.

18 July

"Now Joshua son of Nun was full of the spirit of wisdom, for Moses had laid his hands on him. So the people of Israel obeyed him, doing just as the Lord had commanded Moses" (Deuteronomy 34:9, NIV).

Prayer Point

Moses was a servant of God who was highly favoured by God and was mightily used by Him. When He realised that He was about to die, He imparted wisdom to Joshua so that He could lead the children of Israel. That impartation that came through the laying of hands earned Joshua the respect of the people He was leading.

Wisdom is essential to equip us with leadership abilities and the ability to discern what is good from what is bad—and also to identify the source of conflicts. In order for us to live a life that is alert and prayerful, we need the spirit of wisdom to guide us into all truth and all strategies that will make us come out victorious.

Pray that in areas where you are expected to exercise different roles or levels of authority, God's Spirit of wisdom channel you into excellence as He helped Joshua to lead the Israelites. Pray that the hand of God protects you and guides you and that every move you take will be guided by the spirit of God.

19 July

"Wisdom is more precious than rubies; nothing you desire can compare with her" (Proverbs 3:15, NLT).

Prayer Point

There are so many things that are attractive in the world today. Some people are attracted by cars while others love sports. King Solomon was a wealthy person because when he asked God for wisdom, God gave him both wisdom and riches. Even though he had all the wealth, he could not compare the value of wisdom to any of his material possessions.

King Solomon knew that even if you could have all the wealth in the world, it is the wisdom that you needed to maintain and multiply the wealth. It is the wisdom that will safeguard you against bankruptcy because you will put proper plans in place to look after your wealth.

Make a prayer that God reveals the spiritual abilities that He has deposited in you and the wisdom to use them. Make it your priority to value wisdom as something more important to have; when you pray for a new job, pray for God's wisdom to work on that job and excel at it.

20 July

"The Lord was pleased that Solomon had asked for wisdom" (1 Kings 3:10, NIV).

Prayer Point

When you ask for wisdom, you please God because God knows that wisdom is a priority in many of the requests that we make unto Him. We could easily pray that God helps us with a new car. Without wisdom, you could drive that car carelessly and end up in financial trouble and end up worse off than you were before you had that car. When you ask for wisdom first, God will reveal what you need first before you could even think of having a car. Wisdom will make you have order in life.

King Solomon was blessed because he had the wisdom to ask for the thing that would be pleasing to God. So many of us ask for different things from God and God does bless us with those things but because we sometimes lack the right wisdom to look after our blessings—they get exploited by the enemy.

Many people have been blessed with marriages. As we grow with our spouses, we run out of ideas to nurture our marriages so that it can stay exciting and full of love. It is God's wisdom that we need to prosper in every area of our lives. Let your prayer request be about asking for wisdom in your relationships.

21 July

"To the discerning all of them are right; they are faultless to those who have knowledge" (Proverbs 8:9, NIV).

Prayer Point

When you need to be used by God and be able to tell whether something is good or bad or of the devil or from God, you need the spirit of wisdom that will enable you to discern. Philippians 1:9-10 says, "And it is my prayer that your love may abound more and more, with knowledge and all discernment, so that you may approve what is excellent, and so be pure and blameless for the day of Christ."

It is important that we stay alert through the spirit of wisdom to be able to distinguish between good and evil so that we don't get deceived by the enemy (2 Corinthians 11:14). The devil has gone out to deceive the world and we should pray that God gives us the spirit of wisdom so that we can have the knowledge that would be revealed to us by God.

In areas where you have been filled with uncertainty, ask for God's wisdom and understanding to fill you so that you may have peace of mind, knowing God's plans for your life. Pray for the gift to discern—this is essential in your Christian walk.

22 July

"Wisdom will save you from evil people, from those whose words are twisted" (Proverbs 2:12, NLT).

When you walk in the fullness of God and God has blessed you with wisdom, the way you act toward others will be done in accordance with that God-given spirit in you. Sometimes we associate ourselves with people that we don't fully know and we hope that we will get to know who they really are over time. The world consists of so many people who come from different backgrounds; some people befriend us with good intentions, but others have bad intentions. When you have wisdom, you will be guided by the Holy Spirit inside of you to carefully select the right people to befriend.

God will always direct you through His Holy Spirit to establish relationships with the people who will take you to the next level in terms of motivating you and praying for you so that you can grow spiritually. It is when you lack the wisdom from God that you can move from one deceiving friend to the other who will accuse you of things you never said and cause you a lot of emotional pain.

When I was in primary school, I experienced the pain of being accused of things I never said. As a child, you have a sense of wanting to fit it in with the crowd; whether the crowd is good or bad; all we want is to fit in. My experiences taught me that wisdom is needed to choose friends and maintain relationships.

Even in the house of the Lord, we ought to have that desire for growth and be able to use the God-given wisdom to avoid falling into sin or unnecessary temptations by being able to discern the people that we interact with and the people we choose to confide in. Some people pretend to love us so that they can milk us of our plans so that they can discourage us from fulfilling our dreams.

Prayer of the Day

Dear Lord, I thank you for revealing your gift of wisdom to me. I thank you that, as I begin a new journey in life that will be guided by your spirit, I will be able to handle any person who says unpleasant things that can cause an annoyance. In Jesus's name. Amen.

23 July

"My people are destroyed for lack of knowledge: because thou hast rejected knowledge, I will also reject thee, that thou shalt be no priest to me: seeing thou hast forgotten the law of thy God, I will also forget thy children" (Hosea 4:6, KJV).

Prayer Point

Lack of knowledge can get one into serious trouble. A friend at varsity stopped coming for lectures closer to the exam period because she thought it was a waste of time and she chose to study from home for the exams. At the last lecture, the teacher told us that the exam would consist of only the last three lectures that my friend had missed. Unfortunately, I had no way of contacting her until we wrote the paper—and she failed the exam.

She was so sad that she had studied so hard but focused on the wrong stuff. She was a smart student who could have completed her degree if she passed that course, but due to lack of information and the right knowledge, she failed.

As you dedicate some time to pray today, ask God to help you to be knowledgeable so that you don't fall into the temptation of being ignorant and vulnerable to the enemy's attack. Pray that the knowledge of God be filled in your spirit in Jesus's name.

24 July

"Get the truth and never sell it; also get wisdom, discipline, and good judgment" (Proverbs 23:23, NLT).

Prayer Point

The Word of God is the truth that we need to succeed each and every day. When we do what the Word of God says, we become prosperous and wise in our walk with Jesus. The commandment sums up our responsibility as far as our relationship with God is concerned.

The Word of God says we must get the truth and let it stay inside our hearts and never trade that truth for a lie. In addition, we ought to get wisdom, discipline, and good judgment; by doing so, we would be able to act upon what the truth says.

Draw from Jesus Christ in prayer; ask for wisdom that you may act in his ways and be able to make decisions in line with His thinking and be able to do the work that God is calling you to do.

25 July

"To acquire wisdom is to love oneself; people who cherish understanding will prosper" (Proverbs 19:8, NLT).

Prayer Point

One major benefit of wisdom which comes from God is that it makes you to excel on the good things that you do.

Pray for the revelation of areas where God has imparted wisdom in your life that you may start to operate at a level God expects you to operate. Refuse to live in ignorance, but pray to acquire wisdom.

26 July

"Look, I am sending you out as sheep among wolves. So be as shrewd as snakes and harmless as doves" (Matthew 10:16, NLT).

Prayer Point

The world consists of the good and the bad things one could never imagine. When Jesus Christ left His disciples, He left them with the Word. He is sending them to the world so that they can become sheep among wolves and still be able to do the work that they are expected to do.

Jesus wants us as His disciples to be peaceful in our actions, yet discerning so that we can be able to do His work, exercising caution and targeting the areas that bondages ought to be broken.

Dedicate time to pray—that you may be able to live a quality and fulfilling life. Pray that you utilize the wisdom that Jesus has given you and be able to carry out His work with wisdom.

27 July

"I have filled him with the Spirit of God, giving him great wisdom, ability, and expertise in all kinds of crafts" (Exodus 31:3, NLT).

Prayer Point

God has blessed many people with many gifts such as painting or any form of art. Some of the art that people design are so uniquely made that even if you could think of copying those designs, you would not go far because God has not blessed you with that ability.

I met a certain gentleman who makes beautiful 3-D paintings. When I inquired how he got to design paintings, he said it came as an idea while looking at the sun going down. He got inspired to start doing artwork and has never looked back.

God fills us up with the spirit of wisdom that inspires us to do the things that He wants us to do. It is this spirit of wisdom that we have people who have invented different things such as aeroplanes and cars. We also have people who are specialised in different fields of studies with different skills and abilities. Pray that God directs you to the areas that he has given you unique gifts that you may start using these gifts for God's glory.

28 July

"And the spirit of the Lord shall rest upon him, the spirit of wisdom and understanding, the spirit of counsel and might, the spirit of knowledge and of the fear of the Lord" (Isaiah 11:2, NLT).

Prayer Point

Jesus is the Son of the Almighty God whom God has blessed with so much wisdom and understanding. Jesus is equipped with wisdom and knowledge that He can discern even our innermost thoughts. He knows what our actions will be tomorrow and He knows what is in our minds because He has discerned our thoughts.

Pray that God blesses you with the gift to operate at a level where you will be spiritually alert so that you can accomplish your God-given purpose. Allow the Holy Spirit to take away anything that is blocking you from fully receiving God's wisdom. Refuse to find yourself surprised by things that happen without having you prepared for it.

Allow God to teach you, that you may receive His wisdom that is coupled with knowledge and understanding through our Lord and Saviour Jesus Christ.

29 July

"Talk no more so exceeding proudly; let not arrogance come out of your mouth: for the Lord is a God of knowledge, and by him actions are weighed" (1 Samuel 2:3, ESV).

Prayer Point

God blessed Hannah with Samuel after she was barren for a while. This scripture consists of Hannah's prayer to God after God answered her prayer. She praised the Lord for what God had done in her life.

Hannah's suffered mockery from her rival Penninah. She knew how it felt to be irritated by someone who knows your lack. Instead of praying that God can bless you also, they celebrate your misfortune. Hannah came to acknowledge that God is not moved by proud people or people who think that what they have is because God saw it fit to bless them only and to see the other person suffer.

God loves us all and since we cannot all be blessed with the same things at the same time, we ought to control our tongues and not cause pain to other people. Good actions and humility take you closer to God; pride draws you close to hell. Ask God to help you stay humble.

30 July

"Great is our Lord, and of great power: his understanding is infinite" (Psalms 147:5, KJV).

God is so full of wisdom. Everything that He created, he created out of wisdom and understanding. There is nothing that God has created that He does not understand because His understanding is infinite.

It is time to draw from God when you start running out of ideas to solve problems or situations happen around you so much so that you find it difficult to understand what went wrong. God is great and nothing compares to His greatness and power. Isaiah 40:28 says, "Do you not know? Have you not heard? The Lord is the everlasting God, the Creator of the ends of the earth. He will not grow tired or weary, and his understanding no one can fathom."

I pray that God leads you into victory and his infinite understanding.

31 July

"All this also comes from the Lord Almighty, wonderful in counsel and magnificent in wisdom" (Isaiah 28:29, NIV).

Prayer Point

God is powerful beyond what we could have even imagined. He is full of wisdom that no one on earth can provide. The things that were invented on earth were ideas that originated from above in order to make life easy for us to travel and do other good things that benefit us as His children.

Jeremiah 32:19 says that God's purposes are great and mighty are His deeds. God's eyes are always open to all of us on earth so that nothing befalls us. God is wise and fair and He will reward us according to how we have conducted our lives during our short time on earth.

Invite God's wisdom to inspire your work. Ask God to inspire you to excel with the gift that He has blessed you with so that others can get inspired and long to pray and ask God to bless them in order for His name to be glorified.

Chapter 8

Live a Victorious Life

1 August

"To all who are victorious, who obey me to the end; to them I will give authority over all the nations" (Revelation 2:26, NLT).

The success of our journey in life will not be determined by how we started living our Christian lives; it will be determined by whether our lives ended at the time when were still in the right standing with God. It is often possible to live a spirit-filled life at the beginning of our walk with Jesus, but as time goes by and temptation knocks us down, we often lose focus from the things of God. The most rewarding gift that Jesus is promising is for those people who will obey Him to the end that He will give them authority over all the nations.

Challenges in life can often make us feel that God is absent in our lives. A setback can make you feel rejected instead of drawing near to God. When challenges happen, some people draw away from God and disobey God and become vulnerable to the enemy's attacks. Remember the children of Israel when they were going to the Promised Land, there were times when they would disobey God and worship other gods and this would displease God. This scripture promises that if you remain obedient to God to the end, God will give you authority over all the nations.

As Christians, we will meet people who will hate us so much because of our faith in Jesus. Some will not openly display their hatred, but their hearts would be opposing any good thing that they would see God doing in our lives. We should not be surprised when we are hated because Jesus said that all men will hate us because of Him but anyone who perseveres until the end will be saved (Matthew 10:22).

Disobeying God will rob you of your authority over all the nations. These are the last days where trials and tribulations are everywhere and we need to draw closer to God like never before in order to remain victorious. In the same manner that we obey God when things are going well in our lives, we need to continue doing so until the end of our journey. Our obedience to God should be a continuous act because what will matter at the end is not how well we started our race but how well we finished the race. When Moses was about to die, God took him to a mountain in order to view the Promised Land because Moses would not set foot there. He displayed a lack of faith when God had asked him to speak to the rock in order for the water to come out for the children of Israel to drink. Moses smote the rock twice (Deuteronomy 32:48-52; Numbers 20:11). Disobedience deprived Moses of walking in the Promised Land.

Prayer of the Day

Dear Lord, I know that I have areas in my life where I am not fully obedient to you. I know that there are parts of your Word from the Bible that I selectively chose to obey in order to feel compliant to your statutes. Deep down, I know I have not been obedient to the whole truth. Dear Lord, I repent of my sins and would like to live for you and obey you. Please give me another chance to walk in your ways until the end of my journey, in Jesus Christ's mighty name. Amen.

2 August

"See, the Lord your God has given you the land. Go up and take possession of it as the Lord, the God of your fathers, told you. Do not be afraid; do not be discouraged" (Deuteronomy 1:21, NIV).

Prayer Point

It would be sad if when you get to heaven, God showed you all the blessings that were meant for you during your time on earth that went to other people because you did not take possession of them because of fear and lack of courage.

God says that there are blessings that are waiting for you but because of fear, doubt, and discouragement, you are not claiming them. Other people will enjoy things that were meant for you. It could be a position at work that God wants you to fill but because you are undermining your capabilities, you cannot even apply for the position. God has given you all the blessings; all that is left for you is to take possession.

You cannot live a victorious life through your own strength; you need God to believe and trust in Him because He is the one saying that you must go up and take possession of the land and the blessings that He has predestined for you. This is the season to claim everything that the enemy has stolen from you. Pray to gather courage from God and obtain the wisdom to take possession. Stay obedient and do not be discouraged instead take possession (Numbers 14:9).

3 August

"For the Lord your God is the one who goes with you to fight for you against your enemies to give you victory" (Deuteronomy 20:4, NIV).

Prayer Point

Do you remember the story of David and Goliath (1 Samuel 17)? David was small compared to Goliath but because David did not approach Goliath with the aim of relying on his strength, He was able to kill Goliath.

Sometimes in order to defeat our enemies, we don't need to show physical muscles; we need to use spiritual muscles. The spiritual muscles are our prayers to God, asking for His mercies in our lives so that He can fight our enemies. All you need is to surrender all your enemies through prayer. You may not know all your enemies and the weaknesses that they have, but God knows everything and will fight them for you.

In each spiritual battle, pray that God's presence takes over. Allow God to fight for you and give you victory. Pray that His eye is the one that locates all your enemies and uproots them from all the corners where they come from. It is not by strength or power but by the Spirit of God that we get to overcome (Zechariah 4:6). In Jesus's name.

4 August

"I do not trust in my bow, my sword does not bring me victory; but you give us victory over our enemies, you put our adversaries to shame. In God we make our boast all day long, and we will praise your name forever" (Psalm 44:6-8, NIV).

Prayer Point

Physical weapons do not always bring you victory; even people with the most powerful guns get killed because an enemy can use something that you have never thought of to destroy you. As a child of God, you don't need to trust your own strength or wisdom for protection but on God's protection. It is not always that an enemy must be fought to be defeated; at times, the enemy must be put to shame to defeat him

Pray that God fights the visible and the invisible battles for you. Surrender all the known and unknown spiritual battles to God and ask Him to fight them for you. It is only when God is on your side that you can become victorious—but you cannot do it alone.

Psalm 33:16, 18 says, "No king is saved by the size of his army; no warrior escapes by his great strength but the eyes of the Lord are on those who fear him, on those whose hope is in his unfailing love." You don't need to trust physical weapons to attain victory for God is able and with Him, you can win all the battles before you. God created Heaven and earth through His wisdom. Boast in your knowledge of God through Christ Jesus.

5 August

"You will keep in perfect peace him whose mind is steadfast, because he trusts in you" (Isaiah 26:3, NIV).

Prayer Point

Destruction is what the enemy does to steal our peace. He might throw illnesses or death of our loved ones to get us divert our focus and start worrying and not be able to talk to God. It is important that when destruction befalls us, we take away our minds from the issue at hand and refocus on God for He is the one who fights battles for us.

When your mind is focusing on God, your understanding of the issue at hand will be based upon God's understanding. He will clearly allow you to deal with the issues that are within your control because God knows what you can handle. Even with temptation, God does not allow temptation that is too big for us to handle. 1 Corinthians 10:13 says, "No temptation has seized you except what is common to man. And God is faithful; he will not let you be tempted beyond what you can bear. But when you are tempted, he will also provide a way out so that you can stand up under it."

Pray that God puts your mind to be steadfast in Him and to put all your trust in Him. Whatever plans and wishes you have, He will have them in control for your sake. In situations that stir up your spirit and make you worry and no have emotional rest, pray that God gives you peace as you continue to trust in Him for victory.

6 August

"Watch and pray so that you will not fall into temptation. The spirit is willing, but the body is weak" (Mark 14:38, NIV).

Prayer Point

When Jesus came down to earth, he never neglected talking to God in prayer because He knew that it would be a way that we all need to use to communicate with God for all our issues. We pray for so many things in order for our physical needs to be met.

Jesus taught His disciples to watch and pray so that they would not fall into temptation. He knew that certain temptations trap Christians because we don't spend enough time talking to God and asking for His help.

Make prayer a habit in your life. Pray when you sleep and when you get up. Ask the Holy Spirit to teach you to pray. Temptation may lead you into sin, but pray always that you don't fall into temptation. When you feel your body being weak, pray that you don't fall into temptation.

7 August

"I have given you authority to trample on snakes and scorpions and to overcome all the power of the enemy; nothing will harm you" (Luke 10:19, NIV).

Prayer Point

Jesus has given us the authority to walk on poisonous reptiles, but many of us are still running away from the snake with the authority we possess because it is not exercised. With the authority that we have been given, the snakes should be the ones running away from us.

In order to activate the authority that Jesus has given us, sin must not be a barrier. Our lives or our standing with God should be clean because when it is not, we lose a lot of the privileges that God has blessed us with. We might fail to cast out a demon because the demon could be looking at you as someone who has no Holy Ghost fire and would resist leaving. God has blessed us with a mighty power that even if we were to drink poison we shouldn't die (Matthew 16:18). If we don't fully obey God, we lose the effectiveness to use the power.

Pray that God helps you not to trade your authority for sin. Reclaim all the power that God has vested in you and apply faith in order to do the work that God has purposed for you. Pray that God helps you maintain a righteous life so that you can use the authority given by Jesus so that nothing can harm you.

8 August

"I am the Alpha and the Omega—the beginning and the end says the Lord God. I am the one who is who always was and who is still to come the Almighty One" (Rev 1:8, NLT).

There are many names for God in the Bible. In Genesis 17:1 God is referred to as God Almighty (El-Shaddai); in Romans 8:15 it refers to God as Abba father. Genesis 22:13-14 refers to the God as being the provider and God is referred God the Healer (Jehovah-Rapha) in Exodus 15:26. God is everything to us and it would be such a difficult thing to try to come up with a name that would describe all that He is to us.

God says He is the Alpha and Omega. Alpha is the first letter of the Greek alphabet and Omega is the twenty-fourth letter (the last) of the Greek alphabet. Before everything was created, there was God—and after everything has come to an end, God will remain. I get so much joy and comfort from knowing that God is the beginning because He has been here before we were all created. He is the true and original architect of the universe; He contains all the power. He has the power to create and power to destroy. He has the power to give and the power to take. He has a final say in all matters.

As you enter this season in your life where you focus your mind on God and expect breakthroughs in every area where you have been stagnant, have confidence in God believing that He is all that you need. He is bigger than everything that was and that is today and that will be to come. He never sleeps or slumbers. He sees what is hidden in the darkness and He has the power to bring everything to light. It is a blessing to have a relationship with Him.

If we are sick or diagnosed with a chronic condition, we believe what men say about our conditions and forget what God says. If you believe that God is your healer, who says you won't be healed won't matter because you would have believed God. I have heard of numerous people that were told they wouldn't live long, but God resurrected them from their ailments and they lived. I urge you to listen to God in every circumstance because He is the Alpha and Omega. He has the final say regarding your life and is fully in control.

Prayer of the Day

Dear Father, I thank you for reminding me of your Word this hour that describes who you are. I know that you are a true and living God and you never change. I believe that I will never go hungry for you are my provider. I believe that even if I fall sick, you shall make me whole for you are my healer, I believe that even if someone in my life once spoke death to me, declaring that I won't live long enough. You are my healer. Lead me to victory in all the areas of my life in Jesus's name. Amen.

9 August

"Jesus said to him, 'Away from me, Satan! For it is written: Worship the Lord your God, and serve him only'" (Matthew 4:10, NIV).

Prayer Point

In order to be victorious, we don't need to always go to God and pray and ask Him to help us overcome because we have been given the authority over Satan. Satan has been defeated already on the cross. All you need to do is rebuke the devil with the power that has been given to you through the Word of God, like Jesus did.

When the devil tempted Jesus, He did not negotiate or argue with the enemy. Jesus rebuked the devil with the right weapon—the Word of God. The devil cannot stand the truth that comes through the Word of God. If you meditate upon God's word, you are equipping your mind with the truth.

Pray that the Lord leads you into full understanding of his ways and who He is in your life so that you can walk in victory. Activate your authority by rebuking anything evil that forces its way to you. Remind Satan of the truth that is found in God's Word whenever he attempts to speak lies or deceive you.

10 August

"Jesus replied, 'What is impossible with men is possible with God'" (Luke 18:27, NIV).

Prayer Point

When you are trying to make ends meet through your own strength and experience and everything seems not to show any improvement it can be very discouraging. What is important to note is that when all plans seem to have failed, God starts a new chapter in your life.

God is not limited by the size of our problems or the severity of our hurts and problems. All the things that seem impossible in your life are possible through Him. The knowledge of God is not limited by the complexity of our problems. Jeremiah 32:17 says, "Ah, Sovereign Lord, you have made the heavens and the earth by your great power and outstretched arm. Nothing is too hard for you."

Pray for the wisdom to meditate on this scripture whenever you are faced with a challenge where you feel overwhelmed and you start to think that things won't change for the better. Your problem might seem impossible, but you have a big and powerful God who is there to see you gain your victory.

11 August

"I have told you these things, so that in me you may have peace. In this world, you will have trouble. But take heart! I have overcome the world" (John 16:33, NIV).

Prayer Point

Becoming a Christian does not mean you will live a trouble-free life. It means that you are under the protection of Jesus; when trouble comes, you will overcome because Jesus has overcome the world by the death on the cross.

Trouble will come our way in different forms because even our Lord Jesus Christ never said that we might have trouble. He said that we will have trouble. Trouble will present itself in certain forms; in certain instances, it will be in the form of relationship problems, financial, or health problems. When trouble comes our way, we must stay calm because Jesus bore it all for us on the cross. Romans 8:37 says, "No, in all these things we are more than conquerors through him who loved us."

When overcome by trouble in different areas in your life, remind the devil that you are standing on victorious ground and that Jesus has overcome those challenges for you.

12 August

"The thief comes only to steal and kill and destroy; I have come that they may have life, and have it to the full" (John 10:10, NIV).

Prayer Point

The enemy did not come to earth to do anything good; everything that he is after is in opposition to what God wants. Since the enemy did not create anything of his own, his only option is to steal, kill, and destroy what God has created.

Jesus Christ came to put an end to the enemy's works on earth by giving us life so that we can be heirs of His Kingdom and enjoy the good life through Him. Jesus is the gate and whoever enters through Him shall be saved (John 10:9).

Command the enemy with the authority given to you through Jesus to return everything that He has stolen from you. Paralyse all the evil plans that he has to destroy you or your loved ones in Jesus's name.

13 August

"Who shall separate us from the love of Christ? Shall trouble or hardship or persecution or famine or nakedness or danger or sword? No, in all these things we are more than conquerors through him who loved us" (Romans 8:35, 37, NIV).

Prayer Point

In John 16:33, Jesus said that we will have trouble and we should take heart for He has overcome the world. Even when trouble comes our way, it will not be big enough to stand between the love that God has for us through Jesus Christ. Jesus has conquered it all. He has conquered death on the cross and bought us back to God. Through Christ we are more than conquerors.

In times of serious and desperate need, continue trusting in God. In Christ Jesus, we are more than conquerors. Our faith in Christ Jesus will be tested to determine its strength and will require perseverance during hardships.

Christ Jesus has shown His love by the sacrifice He made in the cross in order for you to experience and enjoy His complete love. You need to accept Him into your heart. This calls for victory in every area of your life. Thank God in prayer for the victory that you have received.

14 August

"Do not be overcome by evil, but overcome evil with good" (Romans 12:21, NIV).

Prayer Point

A boy was shot and killed at school by his friend for no obvious reason. It was not clear how the two started arguing, but the argument resulted in the death of one boy. Closer to the date of the burial, the mother of the slain boy spoke openly of how she forgave the boy who killed her son.

When we have been wronged, the first emotion that comes to mind is that we should get revenge, but that is not what the Bible says. The Bible says that we should overcome the evil in the world by doing good; if we fought evil with evil, we would be promoting evil.

Pray that God demonstrates a life of victory through you that no matter how much evil has been done against you, you return it by some good action. Open your heart to the leading of the Holy Spirit in this regard.

15 August

"For I consider that the sufferings of this present time are not worthy to be compared with the glory that shall be revealed in us" (Romans 8:18, ESV).

When you want to see that things in life come to an end and that no person on earth suffers forever, look for a person who is at least two hundred years old and is alive and still suffering. I have not met such a person. People pass away physically and everything that was troubling them when they were still alive comes to an end.

God's time is surely not our time, but the Word of God reminds us that the sufferings of today do not compare to the glory that will be revealed through us later on our journey.

It is evident that—no matter how bad the circumstances that you are going through—it is only temporary and it shall all pass. At times, it may not feel temporary, but it does not have to feel temporary to be temporary. The enemy could be whispering lies to discourage you. Remember that the enemy is a liar and his aim is to get you deceived. Rebuke him by the Word of God that is sharper than the double-edged sword (Hebrews 4:12). He cannot stand it.

Victory cannot be claimed by inactivity and prayerlessness; it is achieved through the knowledge and practice of the Word of God.

Brethren, meditate upon the scripture the minute you start feeling down in your spirit. Do not let the enemy dominate your mind. Stand firm on God's Word because it is true. Your present suffering is nothing compared to the glory that shall be revealed in you and that is God's promise to you. Believe it; you have no reason to doubt God.

Prayer of the Day

Dear Father, I have lost many battles in my life because of a lack of wisdom. I have lost so many things because I was distant from you in prayer. Lord, I don't want to lose anything anymore. I refuse to give up easily in every battle before I can attain victory. Help me, Lord, in Jesus's name. Amen.

16 August

"No temptation has seized you except what is common to man. And God is faithful; He will not let you be tempted beyond what you can bear. But when you are tempted, He will also provide a way out so that you can stand up under it" (1 Corinthians 10:13, NIV).

Prayer Point

When temptation comes your way and you feel overwhelmed and confused and unsure of what to do, remember what this verse means in terms of the measure of the temptation. God knows what you can handle and what you cannot. Handle the temptation in God's way.

In life, there are different strategies that we use to deal with temptations. It could be that we choose to ignore and the enemy makes the temptation more appealing with the aim of winning. God has given you victory over any form of temptation—and He will provide a way out for you because He knows what you can handle.

Temptation is everywhere. You might feel that being dishonest when accounting for taxes won't do you much harm, but it could be just one opportunity that the enemy is waiting for to destroy you. God has given you victory upon every challenge or temptation. Pray for the strength and wisdom to deal with any challenge that comes your way.

17 August

"But thanks be to God, that giveth us the victory through our Lord Jesus Christ" (1 Corinthians 15:57, KJV).

Prayer Point

When we fail to handle certain circumstances through frustration, we end up losing patience and give up. Sometimes we give up a few steps closer to victory. It is by our own choice when we stop trying because victory is what we have been given through Jesus Christ.

Imagine losing the opportunity to sit for an exam because you were convinced that you would fail the course even before you tried. Jesus did not give us defeat; He has given us victory over all circumstances. Even when our actions may not feel victorious when we act as the Word directs, but we remain victorious through Christ and our faith in Him.

2 Corinthians 1:20 says, "For no matter how many promises God has made, they are yes in Christ." In every hurdle possible, see every failure as a success in disguise because Jesus can turn every bad circumstance around.

18 August

"The lip of truth shall be established for ever; but a lying tongue is but for a moment (Proverbs 12:19, KJV).

Prayer Point

Often we lose our victory because of compromising our Christian values. God has an expectation for us in terms of how we manage relationships and how we speak to other people. We become victorious when we speak to other people in truth.

We may feel compelled to lie instead of speaking the truth more—especially when we feel that by speaking the truth we will appear weak. The truth of God will set us free (John 8:32). Sometimes to come out victorious only requires saying one statement of the truth and all the doors open.

Pray that the Word of God surrounds you and convinces you to speak the truth—even in situations where you may not feel comfortable. Let your heart focus on pleasing God and speaking the truth that will always set you free.

19 August

"For by your words you will be acquitted, and by your words you will be condemned" (Matthew 12:37, NIV).

Prayer Point

Eternal victory can be achieved by considering how many of the good and truthful words we say. The Word of God states that we will be judged on our words; saying good and truthful things will work to our benefit.

Victory in Christ Jesus is what we should wish every born-again Christian to achieve through our wishes and statements. The Word of God says that we should do unto others as we would like them do unto us (Luke 6:31). If we want blessings, we should bless others with the things that we would like to be blessed with.

Ask God to help you think about your words before you speak. Pray over your words so that they may be the words that bind together and not separate and the words that heal and not the words that destroy.

20 August

"When words are many, sin is not absent, but he who holds his tongue is wise" (Proverbs 10:19, NIV).

Prayer Point

When we talk and dedicate no time to listening, it becomes easy to fall into the temptation of saying things that can offend others or the temptation to say things that are not necessarily true or half-true. Sin is present where we have a lot to say; if we limit our words, we become wise. This wisdom gives us victory over sin caused by our own words.

Not every battle is won with words; victory can happen even if you have less to say because God comes in and will speak for you. God is full of wisdom and where He sees that you are attacked and action is necessary to get you out of the situation, he will speak on your behalf through an action or intervention that will bring victory to you.

Ask God to help you claim victory in your life by limiting your words where you see a possibility of sinning against God. Pray for His wisdom that whenever you speak, your words are full of wisdom and life.

21 August

"In your anger do not sin: Do not let the sun go down while you are still angry, and do not give the devil a foothold" (Ephesians 4:26-27, NIV).

Prayer Point

Anger is a thief of victory. When you are angry, you tend to act on emotions and you cannot be rational. Anger can lead one into saying things that are regrettable. God does not want us to become angry for prolonged periods because He knows that the thoughts that we have during these periods are not good thoughts. Anger also prevents us from praying. When you are angry, bad things are likely to come out of your mouth.

The Word of God says we must have victory in all circumstances by overcoming evil with goodness. In anger, you lose the goodness and you are vulnerable to the enemy because He can exploit your state of anger and manipulate your thoughts to even get yourself into worse situations where you can even hurt someone physically.

Obey the Word of God that positions you to victory over your emotions and your actions. God is telling you to reduce the time that you stay angry because anger robs you of the opportunity to live a victorious life.

22 August

"Blessed is the man who does not walk in the counsel of the wicked or stand in the way of sinners or sit in the seat of mockers. But his delight is in the law of the Lord, and on his law he meditates day and night" (Psalm 1:1-2, NIV).

As I started making friends at school, I would sometimes invite some of them to my home. However, the saddest thing was that my father did not approve of every person that I regarded as a friend because he felt that some of those people would not be of good influence in my life. As I grew older, I experienced good and bad friendships that I chose with people that shared a similar vision.

As Christians, the starting point for every relationship is to ensure that the relationship will make us better people and will draw us closer to God. The Word of God is the light and the measure that determines whether something is of God or not. Knowing the Word of God will help us discern spirits or influences that are deceptive because through God's Word you are able to check whether the advice you are getting is out of love or has some evil influence.

The counsel of the wicked can come in different forms; it can be in the form of seeking the advice from magicians or fortune tellers that tell you about their predictions. You may battle to believe whether it is the truth because one thing they will never tell you is that you need to seek God and pray and God can turn things around for your good.

Blessed is anyone who does not take advice from people who do not have God in their hearts. People who do not dwell in the company of wicked people are blessed because they pay attention to godly things. Scripture says that these people are blessed because their enjoyment is in the law of the Lord and those who meditate on God's Word day and night.

Prayer of the Day

Dear God, thank you for your Word and for the wisdom that it gives me. I have believed certain people in the past who did not speak your truth at all times. I have watched TV programmes and magazines that did not represent your kingdom and I have done certain things based on the advice I saw and read from these sources even though they were contrary to your word. Forgive me, Lord, and help me to choose the right relationships. In Jesus's name. Amen.

23 August

"But he said to me, 'My grace is sufficient for you, for my power is made perfect in weakness.' Therefore I will boast all the more gladly of my weaknesses, so that the power of Christ may rest upon me" (2 Corinthians 12:9, ESV).

Prayer Point

God's grace is sufficient to help us overcome or deal with any situation that we come across. Some people were born in poor families but—through God's provision—were able to claim victory over poverty and are living in the abundance of God's provision.

You could have been born with a physical limitation, but that does not entitle you to a lesser quality of life. God's grace is sufficient to work through you so that through those weaknesses you can achieve your victory through Christ Jesus. When you are weak, you are strong because of Christ.

Pray a prayer of victory to overcome desires that may draw you away from God. Pray that you remain focused on the things of God's Kingdom that will lead to eternal life. Put your trust in God—and not on the wisdom of men—so that you remain victorious.

24 August

"But the Lord is faithful, and he will strengthen and protect you from the evil one" (2 Thessalonians 3:3, NIV).

Prayer Point

God is there to lead you into the victory of overcoming the enemy. The enemy will try to bring in situations that will discourage you and cause you to cry and feel terrible but God is faithful (1 Thessalonians 5:24). He will always give you enough strength and will protect you from the evil one.

The power of God gives us victory from the evil one through deliverance. Sometimes the pain we feel as we are attacked by the evil one can make us miss the important things of God and lose focus. From the grace of God, we will be restored—even after that suffering (1 Peter 5:10).

It is not by your own works that you are alive. God is the one who has protected you from the evil one. Thank God for the arm of protection around you and never stop asking God for strength to deal with whatever good or bad that comes your way. Glorify God for His faithfulness in your life—and the lives of your family.

25 August

"Because He himself suffered when He was tempted, He is able to help those who are being tempted" (Hebrews 2:18, NIV).

Prayer Point

Jesus knows temptation because he was also tempted while He was on earth. He is able to assist us when we get tempted. Jesus knows how to overcome the biggest temptation. Hebrews 4: 15 says for we do not have a high priest who is unable to sympathize with our weaknesses, but we have one who has been tempted in every way, just as we are—yet was without sin.

There is no temptation that is so big that Jesus cannot help you overcome. All you have to do is to ask Him in prayer that He helps you maintain victory when you come across temptation—and deliver you in areas where you are suffering due to the effects of temptation.

Pray that Jesus gives you the power and wisdom to overcome temptation and to live a life that will prevent you from getting enticed into sin. In Jesus's name. Amen

26 August

"I can do all things through Christ that strengtheneth me" (Philippians 4:13, KJV).

Prayer Point

Many women and men of God who are seriously taking God's work to another level work so hard and do so many amazing things out of God's power. The power of Christ Jesus gives strength. I visited a church and their ministry was on deliverance. The service started in the morning and ended in the evening. I saw servants of God praying for people to be healed and casting out evil spirits that had kept people in bondage.

It was not by their own strength that they did their work—the strength of Jesus was inside them and was giving them the power, revelation, and authority to do the work of God.

You don't have an excuse for not being the best that you want to be with the gifts that God has blessed you with. You can do all things through Christ Jesus who gives you strength. Activate God's power in you through faith and prayer so that you can do all things through Him.

27 August

"Keep your lives free from the love of money and be content with what you have, because God has said, 'Never will I leave you; never will I forsake you'" (Hebrews 13:5, NIV).

Prayer Point

There are many forms of bondage that deprive people of a life of victory because it has taken control of their lives. There are different forms of bondage such as gambling and drug addiction. There is no freedom in bondage.

When the love for something becomes an obsession or addiction, it takes over a person's ability to think logically and it results in living a life that lacks contentment. Scripture says that we should keep ourselves from the love of money because when you are obsessed with the love of money, you will be tempted to go to all lengths to get the money—even if the route could be evil.

Practice the attitude of gratitude where you become satisfied with the things that God has blessed you with. Trust God to meet your needs in the manner and the quantity He deems appropriate. Exercise patience as you wait to receive wisdom from God.

28 August

"For if you live according to the sinful nature, you will die; but if by the Spirit you put to death the misdeeds of the body, you will live" (Romans 8:13, NIV).

Prayer Point

The more your heart longs for spiritual things, the more victory will come your way. The things that cause a lot of heartache are worldly things that can steal one's attention and focus. When we try to pursue these things, we forsake our relationship with God.

You ought to put to death certain things in life so that you can focus on the things of God. Colossians 3:5 says we should put to death, therefore, whatever belongs to your earthly nature: sexual immorality, impurity, lust, evil desires and greed. Idolatry and putting these things to death entitles us to victory over the sinful nature.

Pray that God helps you remain victorious over the things of the flesh that are robbing you of victory in life. Pray that God helps your flesh to submit to your needs of the spirit that are godly.

29 August

"Saul said to Samuel, 'I have sinned, for I have transgressed the commandment of the Lord and your words, because I feared the people and obeyed their voice'" (1 Samuel 15:24, ESV).

Prayer Point

Obedience to ordinary men becomes a challenge if it makes you move away from the ways of God. In areas where God has set you up for victory, you need to be still and wait upon the Lord because you can forfeit your victory by listening to men.

Even if you have sinned against God and you hope to make it up to Him with burnt offerings, the Lord values obedience more to burnt offerings (1 Samuel 15:22). To obey God is more important than making Him a sacrifice.

When you act out of disobedience, you are rejecting God and His Word. God can feel justified to reject you. Pray that you maintain victory in your life by having God's commandments weigh more than what men tell you to do. If men tell you to kill and the Word of God says you should not kill, then live by the Word of God.

30 August

"But the fearful, and unbelieving, and the abominable, and murderers, and whoremongers, and sorcerers, and idolaters, and all liars, shall have their part in the lake that burneth with fire and brimstone: that is the second death" (Revelation 21:8, KJV).

Prayer Point

Every way a person chooses to live and be influenced by has a destination. You can choose to go with the light or the darkness. The works of the darkness are grouped on this scripture that has specifically named characters of those who are destined for hell.

We ought to be encouraged to conduct our lives in a godly manner. We know that the Word of God is the truth; whatever that is promised will surely come to pass.

The devil knows the truth and all he does is tempt and deceive people. They become brainwashed and end up believing what he tells them. Everyone knows that fire burns and you would do anything possible not to go to hell. It can only be deception from the enemy that makes one not live a righteous life. Pray that God helps you live in accordance with His statutes and to love every person as God has loved you.

31 August

"The Lord is my fortress, protecting me from danger, so why should I tremble" (Psalms 27:1, NLT).

Prayer Point

When the Lord is by your side and He is your strength, whom shall you fear? God is the source of all the power and strength and He is capable of bringing giants down through you. All you need is His strength.

Sometimes we run from situations that need God's strength through us to be solved. It is the strength of God that often has to be transferred to us in order to fight the giants in our lives. God had to use David to bring down Goliath.

God could have decided to send a crowd to fight against Goliath on behalf of the young David, but He wanted to fight that giant through David because all that David needed was God's strength. Allow God's strength to take over your being so that you can fear God more.

Chapter 9

Cast All Your Burdens Unto The Lord

1 September

"For as the heavens are higher than the earth, so are my ways higher than your ways. And my thoughts than your thoughts" (Isaiah 55:9, KJV).

Have you ever imagined how massive the universe is? Look at the detail of everything in it and how it all fits together. God has created everything from flowers to animals; people all over the world look different and speak different languages. God's creativity is beyond what men can understand. Even His ways are higher than we can understand.

When we receive blessings from God, we become happy. When we lose something in life—possessions or loved ones or dignity because of a mistake—it's possible that we start doubting God's presence in our lives or start blaming God. God's ways may not always be something that we understand, but we must understand that scripture is telling us about the greatness of God. When your plan B fails and you have no other plan for the future, God's divine master plan for your life will kick in because God knows what is best for you.

What is it that you are often worried about? Is it that promotion that did not come to you? Are you angry and wondering why God did not give it to you? What if God saw that you would have bad subordinates that would make you so unhappy that you wouldn't even enjoy the position? What if God is preparing you for a better opportunity with more responsibility? God knows what is best for us and will give it to us when the time is right.

If you continue in constant fellowship with Him, He is able to give you wisdom to understand His ways. Blaming God when times are hard won't get you anywhere, but spending time with God will enable you to intimately know God and understand how He works. God has not wired us to solve complex life problems, but He has wired us with enough authority to pray to Him directly so that we can submit all our concerns to him. He knows what is best for us; He knows the cause of every problem. Prayer is the way God hears us. God is our refuge and our strength—and He is present even in times of trouble (Psalm 46:1). Call on His name and He will answer you.

Prayer of the Day

Dear Lord, Grant me the wisdom to understand your ways and thoughts so that I may be filled with understanding. Help me make the right decisions and live a life full of joy and peace. Help me to dwell in your presence at all times and accept any situation that I pray about—even when your answer is no—for I know you do it for my own good.

2 September

"Many, O Lord my God, are the wonders you have done. The things you planned for us no one can recount to you; were I to speak and tell of them, they would be too many to declare" (Psalm 40:5, NIV).

Prayer Point

You may have reached a point in your life where you felt you did not know what direction to turn. Sometimes challenges make us feel helpless, tired, and spiritually lazy. Beloved, if you feel this way, know that it is only temporary. God has good plans for your life.

God has not forgotten about you. He knows your pain and what you are going through. He wants to reveal Himself to you through those circumstances that you are facing. He wants you to believe that you have a better future through Him.

Pray that God may start revealing and confirming his plans for your life. Pray that He helps you perfect your God-given abilities for His glory. Pray that you do God's work with boldness, knowing that God's plans are meant for your prosperity.

3 September

"One thing I ask of the Lord, this is what I seek: that I may dwell in the house of the Lord all the days of my life, to gaze upon the beauty of the Lord and to seek him in his temple" (Psalm 27:4, NIV).

Prayer Point

The Lord is good. If you are after goodness, you will surely seek the Lord with all your strength in order to dwell in the house of the Lord. The psalmist's heart was after God's; he had seen how great God was. He made God the priority in his life and sought the Lord that he may dwell in His house forever.

Yield to God by seeking to hear from His heart when you pray. Allow the Holy Spirit to teach you to pray in a manner that will result in close and constant fellowship with God. Whenever you talk to God in prayer, prepare your mind to receive and be transformed by God.

Pray for yourself and your family and friends to have hearts that are after God's goodness. Ask God to help you develop great interest on the things of God so that you can occupy your thoughts and mind in order to dwell into the house of the Lord.

4 September

"Taste and see that the Lord is good; blessed is the man who takes refuge in Him" (Psalm 34:8, NIV).

Prayer Point

I went through a difficult period in my life and shared the challenge with some of my friends and family. I felt no different or better afterward; I felt as if sharing my burdens opened me up to be judged or criticized. I was seeking refuge in people, but not realizing that they had burdens of their own. I decided to talk to God about my problem and He consoled me in a good way that no man would have ever done.

It is a good thing to have people to talk to when things don't make sense to us. Taking refuge in God is the ultimate choice that every person should do to feel at ease without feeling condemned.

I invite you to pray a prayer of full surrender to God. Acknowledge God's goodness in all areas of your life. Ask God to guide you in all stages of your life and believe that He is God. Everything you have or own will be safe in His hands.

5 September

"My dear children, I write this to you so that you will not sin. But if anybody does sin, we have one who speaks to the Father in our defence—Jesus Christ, the Righteous One" (1 John 2:1, NIV).

Prayer Point

Sin is almost everywhere in the world. We are faced with temptation in most areas of our lives. We may get tempted to lie or say something hurtful. God expects us to be in a position to recognise that we have sinned and ask for forgiveness and repent of our sin.

Sometimes the devil will condemn us and make us believe that we will not be forgiven, but that is not true because Jesus will speak to our father in our defence so that we can receive mercy.

Repent of your sins and believe that the blood of Jesus has washed you whiter than the snow. Believe that God is for you and not against you (Romans 8:31). Pray that the Holy Spirit can lead you into a life of righteousness through Christ Jesus.

6 September

"The name of the Lord is a strong fortress; the godly run to him and are safe" (Proverbs 18:10, NLT).

Prayer Point

There is no problem so big or complicated that God cannot solve. God cannot fail. He is the creator of the universe and everything that is in it. When we face obstacles or challenges in life, all we need to do is run to Him and submit to His authority. He will keep us safe.

Circumstances can scare us and make us feel helpless, but God is forever helpful. He wants us to run to him and call upon His name and we will be saved and protected.

Pray that the name of the Lord Jesus be near your tongue whenever you pray. Seal your prayer by the name of Jesus.

7 September

"But they that wait upon the Lord shall renew their strength; they shall mount up with wings as eagles; they shall run, and not be weary; and they shall walk, and not faint" (Isaiah 40:31, KJV).

Prayer Point

When you buy a new car from a dealership, you will make sure that you take it in for routine maintenance so that it will last a long time. Waiting upon the Lord is similar to a visit to a garage because, as you wait upon the Lord, you wait in anticipation of a breakthrough that God will renew your strength and you will fly high like an eagle.

Pray that the Holy Spirit guides you and makes you more patient in areas where you have been hasty. Ask God to renew your strength where you have been weary and enable you to run your race—even if you feel tired or close to giving up.

Know that when you give up in life, the devil rejoices. When you persevere in trusting God for your circumstances to change, you are defeating the enemy and walking in victory.

8 September

"I am leaving you with a gift—peace of mind and heart, and the peace I give is a gift the world cannot give. So don't be troubled or afraid" (John 14:27, NLT).

When you are experiencing deep pain in your spirit or are afraid that you could lose something dear to you, it is difficult to maintain peace if you rely on your own strength. This scripture tells us that having peace of mind and heart is a gift that Jesus Christ is giving to those who believe in Him. It is the peace that the world cannot give you; it only comes from Him.

I have experienced different forms of hardships. At thirteen, my parents had some challenges and my mother stayed at her parents' place for some time. I had to cook for my father and three siblings, do laundry, and clean the house.

I missed playing with my peers. The strangest thing was that everything that was happening did not steal my peace of mind; I managed to do well at school despite the circumstances. People used to feel sorry for me. An old lady near our house remarked about how much pain I was carrying as a child. That was the assumption because even though I was hurt by my parent's separation, I trusted in God for their reconciliation. God gave me inner peace; I was able to focus and pass my exams with good grades.

The peace that God gives you in times of turmoil is so big that—despite the setbacks in life—you maintain your focus. You still find yourself making contributions to meetings and being able to speak sense to your children. It is not the peace that comes from the world—it is a peace that comes from God. The world cannot give you that peace—your wife, husband, parents, or children will not give you that peace. Only Jesus can.

Prayer of the Day

Dear God, I thank you for your Word because it is life and it is powerful. You are always there to provide for our physical and emotional needs. I ask for the power of the Holy Spirit to dwell in me so that I can work and live in peace. I pray that no matter what setbacks I face, this peace makes me rise above such challenges, in Jesus's name. Amen.

9 September

"Greater love has no one than this that he lay down his life for his friends" (John 15:13, NIV).

Prayer Point

Jesus is not only our Saviour and King—He is our friend. Friends value each other. When we plan an event, we invite our friends to join us.

We communicate with each other quite often and keep our friends informed with progress in our lives. Jesus has done exceedingly and abundantly the things that no ordinary friend would do under normal circumstances. He gave His life for us because of the love that He has for us.

Make Jesus your friend in remembrance of the sacrifice that He made for us on the cross. Invite Him in all the affairs of your life because you need Him. He will be there to rescue you in times of need and will never leave you or forsake you.

Pray that the Holy Spirit leads you to demonstrate your love for Jesus and teaches you to live a life that is full of love and generosity. Allow the Holy Spirit to share the love of Christ with your unsaved friends, colleagues, relatives, and family.

10 September

"And we know that all things work together for good to them that love God, to them who are the called according to his purpose" (Romans 8:28, KJV).

Prayer Point

God created everything—including you and me—with a purpose. He created us to do good works (Ephesians 2:1). We get tempted and sometimes go through tests that we don't understand. This scripture encourages us to understand God's greatness in our lives, knowing and believing that He will never desert us. Every circumstance that happens in your life is meant to change something in you.

Allow God to reveal His specific purpose for your life in terms of your abilities. Be patient and ask God to let His wisdom fill your heart with understanding—even when things don't make sense. He never lies—believe that everything will ultimately work out for your own good.

Pray that the hand of God protects you and guides you in the right direction when faced with difficult challenges. Always remember that His plans are meant to help you and not to harm you—know that everything will ultimately work out for your good.

11 September

"What, then, shall we say in response to this? If God is for us, who can be against us?" (Romans 8:31, NIV).

Prayer Point

It is important to live a life that is pleasing to God in every way. Even when doing business in a corrupt market, country, or industry, it is important to do it in God's way. When God is on your side, nothing can be against you.

Pray that God's favour remains upon you by living a life of obedience that will make Him to stay on your side always. Resist the temptation to look for quick gains without God because those can cost you eternity. It is better to do business God's way and learn patience and perseverance than to get rich overnight through ungodly means.

Meditate on this scripture until it sinks in your heart so that you continue to remember that when God is on your side, no one can come against you. Say this scripture whenever you are faced with adversity and the enemy will flee from you.

12 September

"And I am convinced that nothing can ever separate us from God's love. Neither death nor life, neither angels nor demons, neither our fears for today nor our worries about tomorrow—not even the powers of hell can separate us from God's love. No power in the sky above or in the earth below—indeed nothing in all creation will ever be able to separate us from the love of God that is revealed in Christ Jesus our Lord" (Romans 8:38-39, NLT).

Prayer Point

I have made it a habit in my walk with God to regularly thank God for Jesus because He saved me. I am able to talk about His love for me because God has loved me in a way that is beyond my understanding. God loved us so much that He gave us His son Jesus to die for us (John 3:16). There is no greater love than that.

As part of your prayer today, praise God and tell Him how much you thank Him for your new life through Christ Jesus. God's love is eternal and not determined by seasons or circumstances.

Pray for the renewal of your mind. Always remember that—even if no one has ever told how much they love you—God loves you and He always will. Even if you were rejected by your wife, husband, children, or friend, allow God's truth to dwell in your mind and know that no circumstance will ever separate you from the love of God.

13 September

"Now we see things imperfectly, like puzzling reflections in a mirror, but then we will see everything with perfect clarity. All that I know now is partial and incomplete, but then I will know everything completely, just as God now knows me completely" (1 Corinthians 13:12, NLT).

Prayer Point

Humans were made by God with a power that is sufficient but limited in certain respects. Our understanding of certain things may not be full, but as believers in Christ Jesus, we know that God is complete and perfect. God has given us imperfections so that we can rely on Him for perfections.

Pray that God can bring that understanding to acknowledge that what you see on earth is impartial. We will see a perfect picture when we get to heaven someday. Persevere in prayer and never allow yourself to be discouraged. Glorify God in prayer for nothing supersedes his majesty.

Pray that God may help you grow in knowledge and understanding of your weaknesses so that He can help you overcome.

14 September

"Therefore we do not lose heart. Though outwardly we are wasting away, yet inwardly we are being renewed day by day. For our light and momentary troubles are achieving for us an eternal glory that far outweighs them all. So we fix our eyes not on what is seen, but on what is unseen. For what is seen is temporary, but what is unseen is eternal" (2 Corinthians 4:16–18, NIV).

Prayer Point

When you have been through many challenges in life or you are just persevering in prayer hoping that your painful situation will change, it's likely to seem as if you are wasting your time and energy. Since this challenge is causing you to pray, we know that you are being renewed day by day.

It is often hard to believe that the problems that we face on earth are temporary, but it is important to invite God to help us overcome through prayer. Waiting upon the Lord requires waiting in faith and prayer—trusting God for a breakthrough that will be about fixing our lives on what is unseen.

I invite you to pray that God gives strength to fight for your destiny by giving you the strength to work hard to impress Him in your good deeds of service of love and perseverance.

15 September

"Come to me, all you who are weary and burdened, and I will give you rest" (Matthew 11:28, NIV).

Are you feeling tired of all the challenges in your life? God is commanding you to come to Him because He will surely give you rest. You may be wondering how you can achieve that, but the only way is to go before God through prayer and surrender all the problems that are making life difficult for you.

I lost my father at the age of seventeen and the saddest thing about my father's death was that it was a planned assassination that my Dad knew about. The assassins were planning to have him killed before Christmas of that year. He told my family about it. It was a sad moment for me because I felt helpless and did not know what to do as a firstborn child. I remember dedicating a full day when I was at boarding school. I fasted and prayed that God would stop this assassination, but my dad still got killed. Worst of all, I was the only one who witnessed His killing that night. I saw him take his final stride and gave up his last breath. Although my dad passed on, God was always there to provide for me.

In the midst of it all, God was faithful to me and my family. He gave me the strength to carry on despite the trauma. I believe the prayer I made to God and the fasting I did helped me face the future. I continued doing well at school and God gave me a bursary to go to university that paid for all my university fees. I started knowing and believing in my heart that even though my natural dad was gone, God cares and continues to take care of me and my family. I experienced God becoming the God of the fatherless and the defender of widows (Psalm 68:5) at that time.

No matter your situation, know that God has never forsaken you. God cares for all of us. Take note of this benefit and draw closer to God in times of trouble. No matter how overwhelmed you may be feeling in life, go to God in prayer and faith for His promise is to give you rest.

Prayer of the Day

Dear Father, I come before you wanting to surrender all my burdens unto you because I have realised that I cannot handle them alone. From today, I want to rest in your presence and only think about all the good things that you have done in my life and to start visualizing the good things that you will continue doing for me. You have blessed me in many other areas of my life and even what the enemy thinks he has stolen, you will restore. Forgive me for dwelling too much on the negative. Give me the strength to trust in you in all the circumstances. In Jesus's name. Amen.

16 September

"But what things were gain to me, these I have counted loss for Christ. I also count all things lost for the excellence of the knowledge of Christ Jesus my Lord, for whom I have suffered the loss of all things, and count them as rubbish, that I may gain Christ and be found in Him, not having my own righteousness, that is from the law, but that that is through faith in Christ, the righteousness that is from God by faith" (Philippians 3:7-9, KJV).

Prayer Point

Life in Christ gives us the entitlement to the righteousness that we can only receive in Him because of the sacrifice that He made for us on the cross. As a Christian, our new life in Jesus comes as a result of the grace we have received in Him from the time we accepted Him as our Lord and Saviour.

Pray that God helps you invite Christ to be at the centre of your life. Through Christ, you have been made righteous. Pray that the Holy Spirit expands your thinking into understanding the role of Christ Jesus in your life.

Intercede for the winning of souls to Christ through the realization by other people of God's greatness through the sacrifice that only God could have made.

17 September

"Then Christ will make his home in your hearts as you trust in Him. Your roots will grow down into God's love and keep you strong. And may you have the power to understand, as all God's people should, how wide, how long, how high, and how deep His love is. May you experience the love of Christ, though it is too great to understand fully. Then you will be made complete with all the fullness of life and power that comes from God" (Ephesians 3:17-19, NLT).

Prayer Point

What stands out the most for me is how big the love of Jesus Christ is. To do what Christ did for us on the cross it takes a lot; it takes someone who is so full of love, someone prayerful and humble to stand any humiliation that He experienced on the cross.

It brings so much life and power to understand the meaning of Christ's sacrifice in our lives. He paid the price for us so that we can get the new life through Him.

Pray for the experience of the love of our Lord Jesus Christ in all areas of your life. Pray that God revives the feeling of being loved beyond measure by Him through His son, Lord Jesus, by asking God to constantly remind you of the fact that Lord Jesus dwells in your heart if you trust in Him.

18 September

"Now all glory to God, who is able, through his mighty power at work within us, to accomplish infinitely more than we might ask or think. Glory to him in the church and in Christ Jesus through all generations forever and ever! Amen" (Ephesians 3:20-21, NLT).

Prayer Point

When God calls you to any ministry in His Kingdom, He calls you knowing your strengths and weaknesses. His aim is not to get you exposed or humiliated; it is to transform you to somebody that you were not so that He can be glorified. Moses had speech difficulties (Exodus 4:10), but God saw it fit to use him to lead the Children of Israel out of Egypt.

God's power is at work within you. Do not let anything in this lifetime hold you back from achieving any goal. God knows your weaknesses and He will turn them around and turn them into your strengths for His glory.

Give the Lord praise for who He is in your life. Acknowledge his love and mercies in all areas of your life. Trust Him for the future for He is a faithful and awesome God. Believe in Him for breakthrough in areas when you need them most. Pray without ceasing until you receive the breakthrough. When you feel inadequate, God is always adequate and able.

19 September

"And so, dear brothers and sisters, we can boldly enter heaven's Most Holy Place because of the blood of Jesus" (Hebrews 10:19, NLT).

Prayer Power

There is tremendous power in the blood of Jesus. It is through the blood of Jesus that makes it possible for us to enter heaven through prayer because we pray directly to God.

Plead the blood of Jesus in difficult situations where you see no way out. God will make a way for you. In your walk in life where things remain uncertain, plead the blood of Jesus and have the chains of bondage loosened in Jesus's name.

I invite you to say a special prayer of gratitude to God for the precious blood of Jesus; this has made you qualified to enter heaven. Thank God in prayer for protection, healing, and salvation through the blood of our Lord and Saviour Jesus. Amen.

20 September

"Consider it all joy, my brethren, when you encounter various trials, knowing that the testing of your faith produces endurance. And let endurance have its perfect result, so that you may be perfect and complete, lacking in nothing" (James 1:2-4, NASV).

Prayer Point

It is rather difficult to be joyful when you face trials and tribulation. When we go through challenges in life—it remains important to remember what this scripture says.

When trials befall you after you have received Christ as your Saviour, it could be that the enemy is trying to attack you for the right things you are doing in Christ. The enemy will try to disturb your peace. Include in your prayer, for the Spirit of God to continue strengthening you when you come across trials and that you may understand what trials mean in your life.

When things become difficult, some people don't know where to turn; they easily give up on life without enduring. Pray that God equips you with an enduring spirit that will enable you to stand even in the most difficult times.

21 September

"This is what the Lord says: 'Cursed is the one who trusts in man, who depends on flesh for his strength and whose heart turns away from the Lord'" (Jeremiah 17:5, NIV).

Prayer Point

God answers our prayers in many ways. He may use a colleague or relative as a vessel to get you where He wants you to be. Often, we lose sight of the initial request that we made to God and we don't thank Him enough for being faithful. We lose sight and do the things that praise the vessel that God has sent instead of thanking God directly. If your manager at work has promoted you recently and you know that you have been praying to God for that breakthrough, do the right thing and trust God and not man for giving you a promotion.

Cursed is the person who trusts in man or who believes that by their own strength they made things happen. Without God, there is nothing we can do as humans.

No matter how good you may think you are at a particular craft, always attribute it to God because your strength draws from God who is the source of your talents or abilities. Even when you are sick, don't put your trust in doctors—put your trust in God because He is the source of their wisdom. Without God, no medication would have been invented. Pray that your heart focuses in God always.

22 September

"Give your burdens to the Lord, and He will take care of you. He will not permit the godly to slip and fall" (Psalm 55:22, NLT).

Have you experienced so many challenges in life that it seemed as if everything you tried to do crumbled and you even found it hard to stand? A couple of times we come across challenges that are so huge that we don't know where to begin solving them. Let me tell you, beloved, some problems are not for you to solve but for you to cast and give to the Lord.

God did not design us to handle our own challenges; if that was the case, there would be no need for God in our lives. God is there to solve the challenges for us. All we have to do is remember to cast all of our burdens to Him and trust Him to take care of them for us.

The moment that happens, our mind gets renewed and our strength is restored. Giving your burdens to God does not mean you must give some of the burdens to God. You must give all of your burdens to God because God is—and will always be—bigger than your problems. I invite you to trust God with all your heart and an understanding that there is no problem that God cannot solve because nothing is impossible with God.

Cast every burden unto Lord Jesus; He bore the worst on earth for us. He conquered death for us, the most brutal in the world. Allow him to take care of your worries because he knows how. Crying all day won't solve your problems. Spending sleepless nights will not solve your problems. Casting your burdens to our Lord and Saviour Jesus Christ will free you of all the worries. Pray in tongues if you can and witness the yokes of bondage being broken and be set free. God is a faithful God; He will surely sustain anybody who comes to him.

Prayer of the Day

Dear Lord, teach me how to take all my burdens to you that I may feel lighter and not worry. You said you would never let the godly slip away or fall and I believe you. Make me see your glory in my life, through the transformation of my weaknesses into strengths and through my heightened focus in my life, that I may live a joyful life, in Jesus's name. Amen.

23 September

"This is the Word of the Lord to Zerubbabel: 'Not by might nor by power, but by my Spirit,' says the Lord Almighty" (Zechariah 4:6).

Prayer Point

It is possible to think that in order to achieve big goals, you need to look big. On the other hand, we could think that because you are coming from a poor background, you won't go far in life or achieve much. God is telling you not to look at outside factors; God is all that you need to move mountains and to start seeing miracles happen in your life.

Depend on God for anything in your life through prayer. Nothing is by your might or power. With God, miracles will start happening in your life.

You could be working with difficult people and be so frustrated that you want to leave the organization. Through prayer and faith in God, God can move the mountains for you. He can make those people leave and have you stay—but you have to trust in Him.

24 September

"The Sovereign Lord is my strength; he makes my feet like the feet of a deer, he enables me to go on the heights" (Habakkuk 3:19, NIV).

Prayer Point

Different stages of our lives require a different measure of our strength in order to move from one level to the other. When you attended primary school, you did not need to study as you did in high school. The same is true with being a Christian; as we grow, our strength has to be drawn through prayer and fasting to move to the desired level of progress in our life.

It can only be God who makes it possible for you to go on the heights for it is God who is your main source of strength. I have seen people who were once strong physically—some were even boxing champions—but as they aged or grew ill, they could not rely on their own strength to climb heights. God's strength will make you go to heights that your own strength will not take you

As you pray today, ask God to fill you up with the power of His strength that you can serve in His ministry and be able to go to heights in areas that have been stagnant. Humble yourself and yield to God for strength to overcome and go on greater heights.

25 September

"For the foolishness of God is wiser than man's wisdom, and the weakness of God is stronger than man's strength" (1 Corinthians 1:25, NIV).

Prayer Point

We can never compare our strength to God's strength because He created us. There are so many things that are part of God's creation that men cannot do. No man can create the heavens and the earth, but God has done that.

I just want to invite you to draw near to God so that He can elevate you and enable you to understand His ways and to impart wisdom and understanding in your life. I pray that He grants you the strength that will equip you to make the right decisions, strength that will make it possible for you to love truly.

Submit all your future plans to Him for everything on earth is possible to accomplish as long as we rely on God's strength and not our own.

26 September

"But He said to me, 'My grace is sufficient for you, for my power is made perfect in weakness.' Therefore I will boast all the more gladly of my weaknesses, so that the power of Christ may rest upon me. For the sake of Christ, then, I am content with weaknesses, insults, hardships, persecutions, and calamities. For when I am weak, then I am strong" (2 Corinthians 12:9-10, NIV).

Prayer Point

God is not looking for perfect people to use or to draw near to Him. He wants people who are full of weaknesses so that they can rely on Him for strength. Would you see a need of having God in your life if you could do everything in life? I think prayer in most people's lives would be optional because you would have all you need without praying hard for it. You would have a dream marriage, wonderful kids who don't get sick and are well behaved, and be financially stable. Everything in your life would just be the way you want it to be. A life like that would make one not see a need for asking anything from God because it would always be there.

God has not made people perfect; He made us with limitations so that we can constantly ask Him for help in areas of lack. God's grace is so sufficient that it meets all our needs.

Pray that God helps you to admit and appreciate your weaknesses for it is an opportunity for God to work through those for your sake through His grace for His glory.

27 September

"But the Lord stood at my side and gave me strength, so that through me the message might be fully proclaimed and all the Gentiles might hear it. And I was delivered from the lion's mouth" (2 Timothy, 4:17).

Prayer Point

When we have a new challenging role in God's Kingdom, we need to invite God to stand by our side and watch over us and fill us up with powerful and supernatural strength that will make us soar and do a good job for His sake.

God is waiting for you to invite Him to stand by your side and lead and guide you into doing the things that He has purposed for you to do. He wants you to proclaim His gospel and the gospel is His. You are a messenger for His Word.

Pray that God helps you in finding ways for proclaiming His Word in the way that will make Him have full control by controlling your actions, words, and how you convey the good news so that people can be touched and be healed emotionally and physically.

28 September

"Finally, be strong in the Lord and in the strength of his might." (Ephesians 6:10).

Prayer Point

Strength is always needed before one can embark on any task. To work in a garden, strength is needed. To cook and to do many other things, strength is needed. As Christians, we need to be strong to do the work that God calls us to do. God needs strong vessels and He requires the minimum from us. He will do the rest because God is the ultimate source of our strength.

God expects us to have faith in Him whether or not things are going well. Faith in God is the way we connect with Him. Once we are connected with God, we will be able to do anything that He wants us to do through the strength we will receive from Him.

Pray that your faith increases from where it is to a level that will enable you to maximize your God-given strength for His glory.

29 September

"I am the good shepherd; I know my sheep and my sheep know me" (John 10:14, NIV).

Prayer Point

I have seen God come through in people's lives in ways that no man could have ever predicted. I have seen God make people meet with the aim of building long-lasting and worthwhile relationships only to realise later that it was the Good Shepherd who knows His sheep and what they need.

Jesus knows each sheep and He knows the most nutritious pastures. He will always do His best to take the sheep there. When a sheep gets lost, He will be the first one to notice because He keeps a record of the number of sheep.

Trust in the good shepherd to take you to the right pastures. Just as a sheep does not worry about where the shepherd will take it, you must learn to trust Jesus for your provision.

30 September

"He maketh me to lie down in green pastures: he leadeth me beside the still waters" (Psalms 23:2, KJV).

Prayer Point

David had the privilege to experience the love of God. He felt loved and led by God. God has been a source of peace and guidance in David's life. He appreciated the love of God.

There comes a time in life where you come to a crossroads and you don't know what path to take that will lead you to the greener pastures. You may worry because you cannot trust yourself to predict the path. That's when you need God to come and lead you toward still waters.

From a distance, we often look at things as perfect. When we get closer, we realize that the grass is not always greener on the other side. It becomes a big disappointment and frustration after we realise that we have allowed our eyes to lead us to wrong pastures that only appeared green from a distance. It is time to allow God to lead you beside still waters. God is the one who knows what is ahead of us and what will be good for us. Allow God to lead you.

Chapter 10

Choose to Obey God's Word
at All Times

1 October

"Peter and the other apostles replied, 'We must obey God rather than men'" (Acts 5:29, NIV).

The laws of God and what He expects from us are clear from the book of Genesis to the book of Revelation. God wants us to grow in love for Him by doing good works and by being obedient to His commands. When God took the Children of Israel out of Egypt, He gave them the laws that they had to abide by. Those commandments are meant for every Christian today because God's Word is still relevant. God never changes. In Malachi 3:6, God says, "I, the Lord, do not change. So you, O descendants of Jacob, are not destroyed."

The world has undergone so many changes. In certain countries, Christianity has been abolished. In some of these places, a few Christians worship in secret out of fear of persecution. In certain schools, they don't allow prayers to be held at the beginning of lessons. That should not force us as Christians not to love God because the Word of God says we must obey God rather than men.

There are many ways that we can show obedience to God; one is to live in accordance with what He expects of us. Even if the world promotes violence, we can choose to live in peace. God says we should love our enemies and pray for those who persecute us (Matthew 5:44).

It is important to acknowledge the power of God in our lives and to walk in His guidance at all times. Obey God's commands; the rules given by men could contradict what God expects of us. In certain countries, it is okay to kill. We need to look at what God says regarding murder. Obedience to men could lead to death, but obedience to God will always lead to eternity.

Prayer of the Day

Dear God, I know that in certain areas I have fallen victim to going against your will. I accept that I have gone against your statutes and your word. I have often fallen into temptation of obeying men; I repent of my sins. Please forgive me, Lord. Help me to hear your voice only and be reminded that your way only leads to life and prosperity. Give me the wisdom to know and obey you always. Give me the ability to know what is of you. In Jesus's name. Amen.

2 October

"Ye shall walk after the Lord your God, and fear Him, and keep His commandments, and obey His voice, and ye shall serve Him, and cleave unto Him" (Deuteronomy 13:4, KJV).

Prayer Point

This verse is a summary of our Christian duties and responsibilities. God wants you to take stock of how far you have gone in accordance with His word. Fear of the Lord will make you not wander from His ways; it will make you remember how big and powerful He is.

Your fear of the Lord will make you love Him by looking at the unique person that He has created in you and thanking Him for the person that you are. It is your fear of the Lord that will make you not want to disappoint him; you will do everything that you can to make God happy by keeping his commandments and living your life to please Him.

Pray that through the help of God you may start walking in the fear of the Lord and by being obedient to His commands. Pray that God uses you in the ministry that He has designed you for.

3 October

"If you love me, you will keep my commandments" (John 14:15, NIV).

Prayer Point

Jesus says your love for Him will not be by words without actions. It will be shown by keeping His commands and applying them in our lives. If you live a life that contradicts what Jesus expects of you as a Christian, you are disobeying God.

Let your ways conform to God's commands. Respect the Word of God by doing what the Word says you must do. God's Word says that when we obey Christ's commands, we have come to know who Christ really is (1 John 2:3).

Ask the Holy Spirit to help you live a holy life so that you may remain obedient and stay in God's ways. Ask guidance and understanding as you read His Word so that you may obey His commands in full.

4 October

"Now therefore, if ye will obey my voice indeed, and keep my covenant, then ye shall be a peculiar treasure unto me above all people: for all the earth is mine" (Exodus 19:5, ESV).

Prayer Point

The promise that comes with being obedient to God's voice and keeping His covenant is that we will be a unique treasure unto God above all people. When God says you should love one another as thyself and you do as He commands, you are planting a seed of love and God's treasures will take form within your life.

God is in control of the minds of people and He has the power to influence the decisions of people—even the most rigid rulers. In a situation where you need a promotion but are worried that it might never happen because you feel the hearts of the people in charge won't change, remember that God can change anything and anyone. Continue walking in obedience.

Make God know that you are interested in Him and want Him to reveal Himself to you so that you may follow His voice. Go everywhere He directs you so that you can bring glory to His name.

5 October

"Why do you call me 'Lord, Lord,' and not do what I tell you?" (Luke 6:46, ESV).

Prayer Point

How would you feel if a child called your name with honour and respect but did nothing that showed how they value you as a parent? If you would feel irritated and annoyed, I'm sure it is the same feeling that we cause our Lord when we call Him Lord or Master but we still disobey Him.

When we sing songs of praise and say prayers to God, we should also be making progress in our walk of obedience through Jesus Christ. God cannot be mocked by actions that on the outside portray a message of Godliness but in truth we are not doing what God calls of us to do.

Desire a heart of true praise and worship so that the Blessings of God will follow you. Worship God through prayer, singing, and praise. Ask for His guidance to live a life that is full of obedience and a life that is pleasing to God. Let God help you; do not only to listen to His Word, but to do as the Word says (James 1:22)

6 October

"Not everyone who says to me, 'Lord, Lord,' will enter the kingdom of heaven, but the one who does the will of my Father who is in heaven" (Matthew 7:21, NIV).

Prayer Point

It is of utmost importance as Christians to live a life that is pleasing to God. The life that is pleasing to God may not be pleasing to men. God looks at our inward motives when we go to church and He looks at the heart that is where all the truth for Him resides.

The Lord said to Samuel, "Do not consider his appearance or his height, for I have rejected him" (1 Samuel 16:7). The Lord does not look at the things man looks at. Man looks at the outward appearance, but the Lord looks at the heart.

You don't need to go to church to please other people, but your motives of going to church should be due to your relationship with God. Lord Jesus is warning us to always do the things that are in line with God's will.

Make a commitment in your heart to live a life that is in line with God's will. Pray that your life is righteous before God. Pray that every Word of God that is shared with you may guide you to live in accordance with God's will.

7 October

"But this thing commanded I them, saying, Obey my voice, and I will be your God, and ye shall be my people: and walk ye in all the ways that I have commanded you, that it may be well unto you (Jeremiah 7:23, KJV).

Prayer Point

When we do the will of God and live in accordance to His commands, God promises to keep us well. When you obey God, God finds a way of honouring you as His child. God speaks to us in different ways with different channels to communicate with us—but how obedient are we to His voice?

Sometimes we pray to God to help us achieve certain things in our lives. If nothing happens, we feel sad and start blaming God for not listening to our prayers not realizing it is the disobedience which is hindering our prayers.

I want to lead you into asking God to reveal areas of your life where you have been walking in disobedience. Ask for His wisdom to guide you to live a life that will be in line with His commands so that it can be well with you.

8 October

"Slaves, obey your earthly masters with fear and trembling, with a sincere heart, as you would Christ, not by the way of eye-service, as people-pleasers, but as servants of Christ, doing the will of God from the heart, rendering service with a good will as to the Lord and not to man, knowing that whatever good anyone does, this he will receive back from the Lord, whether he is a slave or free. Masters, do the same to them, and stop your threatening, knowing that He who is both their Master and yours is in heaven, and that there is no partiality with him" (Ephesians 6:5-9, ESV).

The nice thing about doing something for God is that He often wants us to put it into practice with the people that we live with. When God says we should love our neighbours as ourselves, it is because He wants us to understand that love should be shown to the people we live with first. It would not make any sense if we could claim to love God with all our hearts but became selfish and cruel to the people that we live with or were born with.

The same principle of having to practice honour and respect is illustrated by the scripture quoted here. Lord Jesus expects us to obey the people who have some form of authority upon us, starting with slaves who have the responsibility to serve their masters with fear and a lot of respect. The Word of God promises that if you honour your master as a slave and you do it wholeheartedly, you will be rewarded for your good deeds. We are not accountable to men but to God. God is the God of both master and slave; even masters have the responsibility upon their servants not to threaten them.

God looks at how loving we are toward Him by looking at our actions that we demonstrate toward others. He looks at how faithful we are to Him by observing how loyal we are to pay back those people who borrow us money. God also looks at how much we honour Him by looking also at how we honour our parents, those who lead us, and our kids.

Prayer of the Day

Dear God, I ask for your help to live a life that brings honour to you. Help me love those people whom you require for me to love so that my love for you is shown through my actions. Help me show respect to anyone who is my senior or leader in my church, family, or any area of my life with the belief that I will be honouring you as I do that. Deliver me from the pride that can hinder my actions of honour. In Jesus's name. Amen.

9 October

"And have you forgotten the exhortation that addresses you as sons? My son, do not regard lightly the discipline of the Lord, nor be weary when reproved by him. For the Lord disciplines the one He loves, and chastises every son whom He receives" (Hebrews 12:5-6, ESV).

Prayer Point

When we become disobedient and go against the will of God, He can discipline us in order to get us back to the right path with Him. The discipline from God is not out of hate; even this scripture says it is just discipline and not a curse.

The discipline that comes from God gives an assurance that God loves you and He does not want to lose you. In the process of discipline, you may need to work harder and longer to show your seriousness about righteous living; it is imperative to have the courage to persevere.

May God's hand lead and guide you to remain on His ways and to equip you with the wisdom to recognise a moment where you are being disciplined so that you can ask for strength to persevere and never go weary.

10 October

"To discipline a child produces wisdom, but a mother is disgraced by an undisciplined child" (Proverbs 29:15, NLT).

Prayer Point

To obey God, each one of us needs to go through the Word of God and establish the specific responsibilities that are pertinent to our roles.

God has expectations for us as his children and He wants us to obey Him through doing what He expects of us in His word.

God has entrusted our parents to call us to order when they feel we have gone astray. At times, as children grow up, they become more knowledgeable and prosperous—even more than their parents. In that sense, the parents still have the responsibility to discipline their children when they deem appropriate.

Discipline can come in many forms—a talk that highlights areas that are not in order or actions that can be taken to correct the mistake. Pray that God gives you the wisdom to give and receive discipline from the people that God has entrusted with that responsibility in your life.

11 October

"Rebuke not an elder, but in treat him as a father; and the younger men as brethren; the elder women as mothers; the younger as sisters, with all purity" (1 Timothy 5:1-2, KJV).

Prayer Point

In certain communities, elders are still respected for the years they have lived so that the young people can acquire wisdom through experiences of the elders. The Word of God expects us to treat those who are much older than us with respect. If it is someone who is not related to us in any way, we ought to show the same respect that we would show if they were our own fathers and mothers.

God wants us to show respect to everyone equally—regardless of their origin or where they live. We were all made by God and our responsibility to show respect to elders comes from Him.

God expects us to respect young people among us because they are also precious in God's sight. We ought to give them the respect that they deserve.

12 October

"But if anyone does not provide for his relatives, and especially for members of his household, he has denied the faith and is worse than an unbeliever" (1 Timothy 5:8).

Prayer Point

God expects us to maintain our relationships on earth in a godly way. Sometimes it can happen that a family doesn't have the same provisions. Others could be richer in certain areas but suffer from certain health conditions. God puts us with our relatives because He wants us to learn and show love for each other.

The Word of God says that anyone who does not provide for their relatives more especially for those of their own household has denied faith and is actually worse than a believer. God wants us to start demonstrating his love and kindness first to those we live with.

It's my prayer that you may show immerse love to your relatives that you could have neglected due to commitments or other reasons. Extend your hand where possible to provide for them in areas where they are experiencing lack.

13 October

"Don't let anyone think less of you because you are young. Be an example to all believers in what you say, in the way you live, in your love, your faith, and your purity" (1 Timothy 4:12, NLT).

Prayer Point

God has standards for living that guide us in different stages of our lives. In this scripture, the Word of God refers to the responsibility of every believer toward the youth. They are also God's children and have been sent by God.

God expects us to show respect to the youth and not undermine them. He also reminds youth that they should live an exemplary life through their conduct, love, faith, and purity. When you live an exemplary life in speech, conduct, love, faith and purity, you are likely to be respected by those who live around you.

Ask God to help you to see, love, and respect the youth in the manner that God expects you to. Pray that God helps to encourage and inspire all the youth in your community to live an exemplary life of good deeds.

14 October

"For as by one man's disobedience many were made sinners, so by the obedience of one shall many be made righteous" (Romans 5:19, ESV).

Prayer Point

When God put Adam and eve in the Garden of Eden, He wanted them to be in charge and to obey Him. He gave them instructions not to eat from a specific tree, but the serpent deceived them into eating the forbidden fruit. As a result, they disobeyed God.

The disobedience that was caused by Adam since He was the head of the family resulted in sin in the form of a curse that we were born under. Through Christ Jesus, we have been given a new life because He obeyed God—even up to the death on the cross—so that you and I can be saved from the curse. If you have not accepted Jesus, you are living under a curse. When you accept Jesus who bore the curse for us, you are a new creature in Christ Jesus.

Ask the help of God Almighty to live a life of righteousness that is pleasing to Him. Pray for the repentance of other people within your family and friends if you sense they are disobeying God.

15 October

"If you are willing and obedient, you will eat the best from the land" (Isaiah 1:19, NIV).

Remember the story of Jonah (1:1-10) when God instructed Him to go to Nineveh to cry out to that city because their wickedness was too much in God's sight. Jonah decided to run away from God to Tarshish. Jonah was swallowed by a fish and he stayed inside the fish for three days. God instructed the fish to swallow Jonah to discipline him because he had disobeyed God.

This shows that sometimes when we act out of disobedience, God can discipline us as a reminder of who He is in our lives. Jonah was given a second chance to follow God's command. Even when God has given us a second chance to do things right, some of us could fail to get it right.

When God's favour is upon you and you still choose to walk in disobedience, you stand to forfeit your favour. In 1 Samuel 13:14, God appointed someone in the place of Saul because Saul had disobeyed God. Disobedience to God can also lead to forfeiting the blessings that He had promised us—just as the children of Israel who were men of war that disobeyed God. As a result, God could not show them the land He swore to their fathers.

Joshua 5:6 says, "The Israelites had moved about in the desert forty years until all the men who were of military age when they left Egypt had died, since they had not obeyed the Lord. For the Lord had sworn to them that they would not see the land that he had solemnly promised their fathers to give us, a land flowing with milk and honey."

God is a father who wants us to obey Him only and love Him only. God wants to be worshipped by us and we should have no other gods except Him. Disobedience in the form of worshipping ancestors or idols brings a curse (Deuteronomy 11:28, Deuteronomy 28:15-68).

There could be areas in your life that you are struggling with such as sexual immorality, gossip, drug addition, stealing, or lying. God is saying that if you are willing to obey His commands and you are willing to let go of sin, then you will eat the best from the land. God is saying this because He wants to elevate you. He wants to move you to the next level, but the choice is yours. He can only do so if you are willing and obedient.

Prayer of the Day

Dear Heavenly Father, from today, I let go of all the things that are preventing me from eating the best from the land. I surrender my life unto your will. May the Holy Spirit guide me to leading an obedient life. In Jesus' name, I pray. Amen.

16 October

"Make allowance for each other's faults, and forgive anyone who offends you. Remember, the Lord forgave you, so you must forgive others" (Colossians 3:13, NLT).

Prayer Point

God requires us to obey Him in small matters and also in matters that require a lot of responsibility from us. If we obey God in small matters, God will find us reliable to trust in big matters.

We ought to make room for others to wrong us, bearing in mind that we are not perfect. If someone has wronged you with words and you feel that you are in control of your words all the time, it does not mean that you can't wrong anyone with actions. You could accidentally bump someone's car or break something valuable by mistake.

Ask for God's help in your life to make room for other people's faults, remembering that you are not perfect. Ask the Holy Spirit to give you revelation about why the person who wronged you needs your forgiveness.

17 October

"Fathers, do not exasperate your children; instead, bring them up in the training and instruction of the Lord" (Ephesians 6:4, NIV).

Prayer Point

Children are sometimes not able to show how they feel when a parent has wronged them in some way. In many circumstances, they tend to cry if they feel overwhelmed by the disappointment caused by a parent.

This verse says the parent should not annoy or make your children angry. However, the children should be brought up in the training and instruction of the Lord. Children are basically left under the guidance of the parents so that they can grow up the godly way.

Ask the Holy Spirit to help you guide and bring up your children in a way that God expects you to. Ask for the wisdom from God to train your kids to walk in the way that God expects them to walk.

18 October

"Children, obey your parents in the Lord, for this is right. 'Honour your father and mother'—that is the first commandment with a promise—'so that it may go well with you and that you may enjoy long life on the earth'" (Ephesians 6:1–3, NIV).

Prayer Point

Children have a responsibility to their parents or guardians where God has entrusted your parents with the responsibility to raise you as their child. Children have the responsibility to obey their parents and show respect to their parents. God promises a long life and that all will go well with you.

Parents are not perfect and might lead a disappointing life to their children. As children, we ought to have forgiving hearts and be able to accommodate each other's faults.

Pray that God helps you stay obedient even when no one sees or recognizes your obedience. God sees everything—even what has been hidden in darkness. Pray that God clothe your heart with the spirit of obedience to your parents or your guardian so that it may go well with you and that you may enjoy long life and please the Lord (Colossians 3:20).

19 October

"But if they will not obey, I will utterly pluck up and destroy that nation, saith the Lord" (Jeremiah 12:17, KJV).

Prayer Point

Disobeying God causes Him to become angry. He could even decide to destroy a nation if people disobeyed as He did with Sodom and Gomorrah (Genesis 19). God wants us to honour Him as our only Creator and God.

There are many sins that are influenced by the places where we live. If one does not read the Bible and live a life in accordance with the Word of God, it becomes a challenge to live a Holy life in a world that is so full of sin.

God can save a whole nation because of a few obedient people. No matter what part of the earth you live in, pray that you obey God's commands at all times. Pray that you continue obeying God—even when no one around you seems to be obeying God.

20 October

"In this same way, husbands ought to love their wives as their own bodies. He who loves his wife loves himself. After all, no one ever hated their own body, but they feed and care for their body, just as Christ does the church" (Ephesians 5:28-29, NIV).

Prayer Point

Husbands have the responsibility to their wives to love their wives as their own bodies. The Word of God is clear; it does not say men should criticize their wives or compare their wives with other women. It says they should love their wives as Christ loves the church.

When you love your wife as God expects of you, you are living in obedience to God—that is what God expects from you. Husband and wife ought to be one thing; hence, the responsibility to love the wife as their own body.

Ask God to help you show love to your spouse and the respect that is expected. Repent of your sins if you feel you have lived a life that caused a lot of pain to your spouse or you knew that you were not obedient to God's Word.

21 October

"Let this mind be in you, that was also in Christ Jesus: who, being in the form of God, thought it not robbery to be equal with God: But made himself of no reputation, and took upon him the form of a servant, and was made in the likeness of men: And being found in fashion as a man, he humbled himself, and became obedient unto death, even the death of the cross" (Philippians 2:5-8, KJV).

Prayer Point

Lord Jesus is our role model and an example of the way in that we ought to live our lives and be exemplary to others. Jesus knew that He was a King, but He did not mention His status everywhere He went. He knew that He was on earth to accomplish a mission that would make

His name glorified forever. Jesus remained humble and obedient until His death on the cross.

I wonder how many of us would remain obedient to God when faced with suffering that would ultimately lead to death. Lord Jesus was the Son of God who knew the Father and understood the benefits that would come through his obedience that led to us being saved.

Pray for the spirit of humility and obedience to control your walk in God. Pray that your mind gets aligned to Christ's so that you may see it a privilege to serve just as Jesus did while He was on earth. Pray that you may remain as humble and obedient as Lord Jesus.

22 October

"'You and Aaron must take the staff and assemble the entire community. As the people watch, speak to the rock over there, and it will pour out its water. You will provide enough water from the rock to satisfy the whole community and their livestock.' So Moses did as he was told. He took the staff from the place where it was kept before the Lord. Then he and Aaron summoned the people to come and gather at the rock. 'Listen, you rebels!' he shouted. 'Must we bring you water from this rock?' Then Moses raised his hand and struck the rock twice with the staff, and water gushed out. So the entire community and their livestock drank their fill. But the Lord said to Moses and Aaron, 'Because you did not trust me enough to demonstrate my holiness to the people of Israel, you will not lead them into the land I am giving them!'" (Numbers 20:8-12, NLT).

Moses was instructed by God to speak to the rock so that the rock could release the water so that the Children of Israel could have water to drink. Moses disobeyed God and struck the rock twice and God was not pleased with His action. Even though God had planned for Moses and Aaron to lead the children of Israel to the Promised Land, He changed His mind and told them that because they did not trust Him enough, they would not enter the Promised Land. Moses was a servant of God who was mightily used by God but toward the end of his journey, he disobeyed God. God had walked with Moses all this time and had used Moses to perform many miracles. God caused the plagues that ultimately made Pharaoh release the Children of Israel, but Moses failed to get it right and disappointed God.

The Children of Israel were always complaining to Moses. Moses was angry at them because they were moaning about water. His actions were definitely made out of anger and lack of patience. Moses probably thought that hitting the rock would be quickest instead of speaking to the rock. This shows that sometimes we disobey God due to anger caused by the people around us. We fail to honour God's commands. Whether your disobedience was as a result of your own doing or you were led to disobedience, it can still cost blessings.

You could be in a journey where God is taking you to the Promised Land. He may have taken you through many life-threatening situations. He has provided for your manna in the midst of major financial needs where you had no way to save yourself. God is saying He is the same God that protected and provided for you yesterday and you have no reason to start doubting Him now. Continue obeying Him and He will see you through. Encourage others who are the blink of giving up. Ask God to reveal Himself to them and to speak to them so that they can stay obedient to His ways and voice.

Prayer of the Day

Lord I want to live my life pleasing you. I know that sometimes I doubt your presence and go astray. I know that I shouldn't do so for I have no reason to doubt you Lord. You have been good to me and I trust you with my life and my needs. Strengthen me, Lord, to stand by your Word and the promises it contains regarding obedience. In Jesus's name, I pray. Amen.

23 October

"And Samuel said, Hath the Lord as great delight in burnt offerings and sacrifices, as in obeying the voice of the Lord? Behold, to obey is better than sacrifice, and to hearken than the fat of rams" (1 Samuel 15:22, KJV).

Prayer Point

There is nothing wrong with giving offerings and tithes to the Lord as long as we know that it is part of our responsibilities as Christians, but this should not be to make up for our disobedience in certain areas. We cannot fool God by living a life of complete disobedience and hope that when God sees our money, He will not worry about our other sins.

To obey God is better than any form of sacrifice that we can ever give to God. God looks at the heart that honours him. God is not impressed by someone who disobeys Him by stealing and bringing the money back to the Lord as tithes and offering because obedience to God is better than sacrifice.

Pray that you remain obedient even when tempted. Decide in your heart to seek obedience in all the things that God wants you to obey Him. Seek to do the things that are important for your relationship with God.

24 October

"Let us hear the conclusion of the whole matter: Fear God, and keep his commandments: for this is the whole duty of man" (Ecclesiastes 12:13, AKJV).

Prayer Point

The writer of the book of Ecclesiastes appears to have observed a lot of the good and the bad that happened in the world. He ended up putting his conclusions down in the book and admitting in certain verses that some of the things he observed were meaningless to him. In the last chapter of his book, he concluded that we ought to fear God and keep his commandments because if we do this, we have done everything.

As you grow and want to know more and more of Christ, we may end up wondering what His purpose for our lives is. Before we can even get to know the purpose for our lives, we need to know how we can fully obey God.

Make a commitment to God to be obedient to His commands and aim to walk on His ways without making exceptions for deviations in all the days of your life. Pray for His help in keeping the commandments and doing His will.

25 October

"If you fully obey the Lord your God and carefully follow all His commands I give you today, the Lord your God will set you high above all nations on earth" (Deuteronomy 28:1, NIV).

Prayer Point

God expects children to obey their parents so that they may have a long life and that it could be well with them. This commandment is for everyone because God is our Father. As children, we owe Him the same obedience. God expects us to obey his voice, obey His commandments, and walk in His ways so that He can set us high above all nations on earth.

You cannot expect to get the blessings of God when God asks you to go to Nineveh and you decide to go to Tarshish, like Jonah did. God wants us to respect Him by obeying His voice and doing as He commands us to do. Just as you would like a child to obey you when you request that they do something for you.

Make it your priority to obey the voice of God that can come to you in different forms. God says something in order for us to act on it. God does not say things for the sake of saying things; He wants us to act and obey His voice.

26 October

"Train up a child in the way he should go: and when he is old, he will not depart from it" (Proverbs 22:6, KJV).

Prayer Point

Children are from God. Parents have been entrusted with the responsibility to look after children and guide them in the way they should go. There are many evil influences in the form of television, radio, and the Internet. The music that is played nowadays many of it contains vulgar and full of evil influence. Guidance is sought for children in this age.

The memory of the things that happen when we are young impacts our view as we grow older. If a good foundation is laid on children's hearts by parents, then children will go on their lives having a strong foundation and won't turn from it.

Start guiding children in your area of influence so that they get to build their lives on strong family principles—even when they are older, they won't turn from it. Ask for wisdom from God that you may guide your children and the children that have been put in your care so that they can grow with the foundation that comes from God.

27 October

"Obey your spiritual leaders, and do what they say. Their work is to watch over your souls, and they are accountable to God. Give them reason to do this with joy and not with sorrow. That would certainly not be for your benefit" (Hebrews 13:17, NLT).

Prayer Point

You could be a member of a church where you feel the leadership of the church is not doing enough to take the church to another spiritual level. As a result, when the leadership of the church puts certain requests among the members, you don't feel encouraged to comply. God has put you in that church for a reason and He does not want you to whine about things going wrong. He wants to use you to take that church into another level.

God wants to humble your heart and get you to have confidence in your church leaders. God wants you to submit to their authority because they were put there by God to watch over you.

Allow God to humble your heart and see the benefits of working with your leaders at church—or in any area of your life—because they were entrusted in those positions with a certain expectation. Your confidence and submission will encourage your leaders to do their work with joy.

28 October

"Wherefore, my beloved, as ye have always obeyed, not as in my presence only, but now much more in my absence, work out your own salvation with fear and trembling" (Philippians 2:12, KJV).

Prayer Point

When you obey God, your level of obedience should be consistent. You must never render a service unto God because you want to impress the people around you.

The Apostle Paul was reminding the Philippians of the importance of obedience. They need to continue doing unto the Lord with fear and trembling even in Paul's absence.

Ask God to help you obey His voice and His commands in a way that benefits and gets you rewarded by Him. Pray that God helps you to stay obedient to His voice and His statutes.

29 October

"As obedient children, do not conform to the evil desires you had when you lived in ignorance" (1 Peter 1:14, NIV).

Prayer Point

We often get involved in so many activities that are often not godly before we receive Christ into our lives. Our behaviour could be such that it conforms to the worldly standard, such as using vulgarities or dressing in a way that is not exemplary to our new life in Christ. When we receive Christ, our old self and habits that we had when we were living in ignorance dies.

As new and obedient children in Christ, we ought to conform to the new way of behaving through Christ Jesus. The desires we had that were of the lustful nature should die in us so that the righteousness of Christ can be revealed.

Pray that God Almighty helps you overcome the desires of your past. Ask God to deliver you, cleanse you, and make you whole. Resist the temptation to go back to the desires that kept you in bondage before you met Christ.

30 October

"But Jeremiah said, They shall not deliver thee. Obey; I beseech thee, the voice of the Lord, that I speak unto thee: so it shall be well unto thee, and thy soul shall live" (Jeremiah 38:20, KJV).

Prayer Point

When King Zedekiah saw that the Babylonians were going to hand him over to the Jews, he became afraid because he thought that they would ill treat Him. Jeremiah asked him to obey God through the Word that Jeremiah would speak to Him—and it would be well with him.

You could be faced with a situation where you feel you could just run away or hide because you fear that if you stay where you are, things are never going to improve. God has confirmed His position regarding this matter, but you are still facing doubt. God is telling you it will be well—just believe and obey God.

God is always speaking to us through His Word and his servants. All we need to do is listen to God and obey His Word; everything in our lives will be well and we shall live.

31 October

"By faith, Abraham, when called to go to a place he would later receive as his inheritance, obeyed and went, even though he did not know where he was going" (Hebrews 11:8, NIV).

Prayer Point

Abraham was a man who walked by faith and not by sight. He trusted God with all His heart and He believed God for even the blessings that would come after He had died.

In Genesis 12:1 the Lord said to Abraham, "Leave your country, your people, and your father's household and go to the land I will show you." Abraham chose to obey God and left his country by faith. Abraham lived for God; when God asked Him to do something, he would do so without asking many questions.

Sometimes we remain stagnant in our lives because of a lack of faith in God. When God has revealed the path you should take and you still doubt His Word, it costs you your inheritance in God. When God sends you, learn to obey; He knows where He is sending you and He will provide for you.

Chapter 11

Be a Cheerful Giver

1 November

"But remember the Lord your God, for it is he who gives you the ability to produce wealth, and so confirms his covenant, that he swore to your forefathers, as it is today" (Deuteronomy 8:18, NIV).

When God gives us the ability to produce wealth, we have the responsibility to remember Him and thank Him for the blessing He has given us. God is not after our wealth and is not interested in getting us payback for each and every thing that He blesses us with. He wants us to learn some good habits of gratitude whenever we are blessed and obey Him.

In every family, when the parents have done something for a child, they expect the child to say thank you. How a child chooses to thank the parents varies. In certain instances, just going back to the parents to say thank you would be enough, but in another family, taking a responsibility to fulfil a particular chore would also suffice.

There are so many ways that one can show gratitude to God for His provision. You can remember God by giving to the church in the form of offerings or tithing. You can offer a lending hand to the poor and be blessed some more (Proverbs 22:9).You can also remember God by giving to the orphans or poor people around you. God is more than wealthy; hence He can bless you with an ability to produce wealth. He is merely testing how obedient you can be after He has blessed you. When God sees that you are obedient, He blesses you even more. The more you give, the more blessed you become.

God is a generous father and He expects us to be as generous as He is. He wants us to learn to give so that we can give on His behalf through the sharing of His blessings that we possess.

Prayer of the Day

Dear Heavenly Father, you have blessed me in so many ways. Thank you for blessing me. I pray that you give me the ability to remember you in times of harvest. Lead me in the direction where I can lend a helping hand to others in remembrance of your provision and your mercies to me. In Jesus's name Amen.

2 November

"In everything I showed you that by working hard in this manner you must help the weak and remember the words of the Lord Jesus, that He Himself said, 'It is more blessed to give than to receive'" (Acts 20:35, NASV).

Prayer Point

To give is more important than to receive. When you part with something, a vacuum is left that makes it easier for God to actually want to fill that vacuum. However, when you are saturated with things that you have been receiving but not making a way out in the form of giving to others, it becomes difficult to continue receiving.

Jesus said it was more important to give than to receive because He was speaking from experience. He gave up His life on the cross in order for us to be saved. He knew the peace of mind that came with giving someone something that they cherish.

When you give from a heart that is willing to give, God is going to bless you. Your attitude has to be right and willing for the giving to bear fruit. Ask the Lord to open your heart to giving.

3 November

"Give generously to him and do so without a grudging heart; then because of this the Lord your God will bless you in all your work and in everything you put your hand to" (Deuteronomy 15:10, NIV).

Prayer Point

When you are generous, you don't become concerned about the quantity of your gifts because you just give in accordance with your heart. What I also find beneficial when faced with a need to give is to pray for my gift and release it in the spirit so that the recipient can be blessed as they receive the gift.

Giving may seem like the person who is more blessed is the receiver, but it is the giver. Your heart has to be open to releasing your gift, trusting that God will bless you as you give in a manner that you have never imagined.

Pray that God gives you the ability to give generously with a heart that is prepared to give and receive from the Lord. God relies on our gifts to bless others. In order to do that, He needs our understanding on the aspect of giving.

4 November

"Every man shall give as he is able, according to the blessing of the Lord your God that He has given you" (Deuteronomy 16:17, ESV).

Prayer Point

One can only give what one can afford. Sometimes when it is a thanksgiving season in a church, people bring different gifts to God according to what they are able to give to God at the time. Some people bring many gifts in accordance with the measure of blessing that God has blessed them, but others bring little.

Whether you give too much or too little is not for men to judge but God. God knows the depth of our pockets. Pray that you give to God what you are able to give at the time. God sees your heart and what you are able to give.

God expects you to give what you are able to give. The decision regarding how much to give normally vests upon you in accordance with what God has blessed you with. Pray that God helps you to identify the possessions that you need to start giving to others and give cheerfully.

5 November

"He who is kind to the poor lends to the Lord, and he will reward him for what he has done" (Proverbs 19:17, NIV).

Prayer Point

There are poor people in many parts of the world. They could be your neighbours, relatives, family, friends, or people who you fellowship with at your church. Poor people are everywhere; God expects us to give to people less fortunate than us on His behalf.

It is not our call to question why a beggar on the street can't go and apply for a social grant or ask for food from His own relatives. It is our responsibility to show the beggar some love and kindness and give wherever we can.

God will reward you for any form of kindness that you have shown to any poor person that you come across. Pray that God helps you show kindness to people who are in need and to show them love.

6 November

"Then the people rejoiced because they had offered so willingly, for they made their offering to the Lord with a whole heart, and King David also rejoiced greatly" (1 Chronicles 29:9, ESV).

Prayer Point

When we were still young, I enjoyed asking for chips from my baby brother whenever mom bought him chips only. He would always give, but few seconds later, he would start crying and wanting his chips back because He had not given me those chips with his whole heart.

When we give to God out of compulsion due to the pressure in our church or somewhere else, we lose out the blessings from God because we are not offering wholeheartedly.

Pray that when faced with an opportunity to offer to the Lord, you do it wholeheartedly so that God receives your gifts and you can be filled with the joy. Acknowledge that whatever you have, your possessions are there because God has blessed you with them. When you give something to God, give it wholeheartedly. God has blessed you with it and make sure that you give God the best.

7 November

"Now this I say, he who sows sparingly will also reap sparingly, and he who sows bountifully will also reap bountifully. Each one must do just as he has purposed in his heart, not grudgingly or under compulsion, for God loves a cheerful giver. And God is able to make all grace abound to you, so that always having all sufficiency in everything, you may have an abundance for every good deed" (2 Corinthians 9:6-8, NASV).

Prayer Point

Giving is a service that is not more for God's benefit but for your benefit. When you have a big farm to sow and decide to just use few seeds to plant in a small section of your farm, you can be guaranteed to receive a small harvest.

When you sow generously, then you will reap generously. When you sow sparingly, then sparingly will you reap. God expects us to generously give with a heart that is free to do so—and in accordance with what one is able to give.

Pray for God to help you give generously in areas where you struggle to extend your hand to give. If you plant a harvest with few seeds, only few plants will grow. If you scatter lots of seeds in a big area, more plants will grow—leading to more harvest. Pray that God loosens your heart into giving.

8 November

"At Caesarea there was a man named Cornelius, a centurion in what was known as the Italian Regiment. He and all his family were devout and God-fearing; he gave generously to those in need and prayed to God regularly. One day at about three in the afternoon he had a vision. He distinctly saw an angel of God, who came to him and said, 'Cornelius!' Cornelius stared at him in fear. 'What is it, Lord?' he asked. The angel answered, 'Your prayers and gifts to the poor have come up as a memorial offering before God. Cornelius has given so much to the poor since he was a God-fearing man. It came naturally for him to give because his mind was in line with what God wanted him to do and that was to bless others through what God has blessed him with (Acts 10:1-4, NIV).

You may not understand what happens when you give or why you have to give, but God wants you to continue giving with a cheerful heart because you are doing it for yourself than for the other person. When you bless someone with a beautiful watch or flowers, imagine God taking that and putting it as a remembrance of your works. When you get to heaven someday, you will be amazed to be shown a room that has stored all the gifts you have given to others that God has kept as a memorial. Wouldn't it be great to have a memorial that is made of things that are new and admirable instead of making a memorial to God of things that you don't want but are simply giving because you want to get rid of them?

Cornelius was a God-fearing man who knew that he was God's servant. Whatever he had, he felt the need to always give because he knew the source of his blessings. Cornelius knew that God's power and provision made it possible to get wealth; further, his mind was in line with God's for He feared the Lord.

God has blessed each and every person with a unique gift. That gift can be shared with others. Some people use the gifts to sing and you can use that gift to sing to raise money for the needy through a concert. God has blessed us in order to bless others who are in need. All we need to do is to give cheerfully and make sure that we give God the best.

Prayer of the Day

Dear God, from today, I will give with an understanding that whatever I give will be used as a memorial to you as it happened with the gifts that Cornelius gave. Help me, Lord, to give with a cheerful heart and to give the best that I can give. Thank you, Lord, because what I have asked for now, I believe I have been granted, in the name of Jesus, Amen.

9 November

"Do not withhold good from those to whom it is due, when it is in your power to do it" (Proverbs 3:27, NASV).

Prayer Point

In positions of power where God places you, He places you with the aim of having you be a blessing to whomever you work with—be it your principals or subordinates. When subordinates work hard to deserve a good salary increase or a good performance bonus, whatever the reward, we should not withhold the blessing if it is in our power to bless.

God wants us to be aware of the good deeds that others are doing around us. If it is within our power to give them the recognition, God wants us to give the recognition to the deserving people.

Let your prayer be that God may open your heart of compassion that you may be able to give where there is a need for you to do. If someone has done something good, reward them as expected because God will take care of you when it's your turn.

10 November

"There is one who scatters, and yet increases all the more, and there is one who withholds what is justly due, and yet it results only in want. The generous man will be prosperous, and he who waters will himself be watered (Proverbs 11:24-25, NASV).

Prayer Point

The attitude of withholding something that is justly due to someone is not godly. God expects us to practice fairness in life and not exercise punishment—even where punishment is not deserved. When you have a worker who should be paid at the end of a particular time and has done what has been expected, then the master should not withhold the salary or other benefits that go with it.

The Word of God says that if anyone withholds what is justly due, they will suffer from lack. What you are withholding will make you poor. If you generously give, God will make you prosperous.

Plant good seeds and expect God to multiply your seeds and increase your harvest. Invite God to bless your seeds as you plant in different areas. If you plant a seed of monetary value, expect a multiplication of that seed.

11 November

"Now he who supplies seed to the sower and bread for food will supply and multiply your seed for sowing and increase the harvest of your righteousness" (2 Corinthians 9:10, NASV).

Prayer Point

God is responsible for supplying us with the blessings in our lives. He expects us to be obedient by planting the seeds so that He can keep on multiplying them for us. Some people wonder why they just don't seem to live in abundance; they forget that they are not planting seeds that God can multiply.

When God gives you a fruit, the fruit is big enough to eat, but the seeds should be left so that they can be sown for more fruit. Sometimes people tend to eat the fruit and the seed and are left with nothing to sow.

Jehovah Jireh is your provider and everything that you have comes from Him—beginning with your own life. God expects you to be generous; He is a generous God and you will have a prosperous life because He will increase your harvest of righteousness when you plant good seeds.

12 November

"All day long he craves and craves, but the righteous gives and does not hold back" (Proverbs 21:26, ESV).

Prayer Point

A righteous person does not withhold a blessing from others. Righteousness comes from within a person's heart and is revealed through our actions. When Jesus was approached by people to be healed, he did not refuse to heal them because He was righteous. He freely healed the sick and did not hold back.

Many people claim to be Christians and righteous, but they require some form of payment in order to pray for you. The Word of God is clear in this scripture because the righteous give and do not hold back.

Ask God to open your mind and willpower so that you may aim for righteousness and be in a better position to give. Aim to give without feeling the pain or loss of whatever you are giving. Giving is an opportunity to be blessed.

13 November

"Moreover, as you Philippians know, in the early days of your acquaintance with the gospel, when I set out from Macedonia, not one church shared with me in the matter of giving and receiving, except you only; for even when I was in Thessalonica, you sent me aid again and again when I was in need. Not that I am looking for a gift, but I am looking for what may be credited to your account" (Philippians 4:15–17, NIV).

Prayer Point

In every church, there are different needs that must be met in order to continue spreading the gospel of Jesus Christ. The servants of God who are full-time in ministry have specific needs that need to be met in order to carry on God's work. God expect us to provide gifts to the servants of God like the gifts that the Philippians sent to Paul.

As we give to the servants of God, we may not feel as if we are giving to God but we are. We are basically making deposits into our heavenly accounts. We should never get tired of contributing in the house of the Lord in order for God's church to grow and not lack.

Identify servants of God in your local church or in other churches so that you may bless by giving them good gifts. God will see your good works and bless you accordingly and your heavenly account of blessings will also increase.

14 November

"Suppose a brother or sister is without clothes and daily food. If one of you says to him, 'Go, I wish you well; keep warm and well fed,' but does nothing about his physical needs, what good is it" (James 2:15–16).

Prayer Point

I attended a prayer meeting where a group member had an urgent need for financial assistance. She needed money so desperately—and she needed to raise the money within two days to settle the debt. The lady was prayed for, but no one gave her any form of financial assistance. It was because of this that I took the initiative to ask for donations from the group in order to help meet the financial needs of our sister because she had been praying as well. We are part of the solution by providing wherever we could.

Ask God to speak to your heart in order to differentiate between the spiritual needs or needs of provision so that you can help whenever you can. If you happen to have clothes that you don't need, there is always someone who is without that you can give to.

Before you throw away fresh food, think of someone you can help before you completely dispose of it because it could be someone not far from you who is waiting for the Lord to answer.

15 November

"But when you give to the poor, do not let your left hand know what your right hand is doing, so that your giving will be in secret; and your Father who sees what is done in secret will reward you" (Matthew 6:3-4, NIV).

Have you ever wondered why God wants people to give in secret? God wants us to give in secret because He wants us to give with the right motive, knowing that we are not giving to impress other people but we are giving to Him only. Have you ever gone to a party with a small gift and noticed other invited people with bigger, expensive gifts? You might wish that you had bought the bigger gift; as a result, you end up feeling like your gift is inadequate.

Giving to God must be done in secret. We should not boast about our tithes, offerings, or any type of gift that we give to God. In the process, we could discourage others who can only afford to contribute the little that they have. Giving is not unto men; but it is unto God.

It is my prayer that we always remember to give in secret because God wants our motive of giving to be right. God wants us to know at all times that we are giving to Him and not unto man so that He can bless us. If we give with a boastful attitude, wanting the whole world to know about the gifts we made to the poor, the only benefit we will have is admiration or envy from people and we will not obtain a reward from God (Matthew 6:1-4).

Prayer of the Day

Dear God, let my motive for giving unto you be right in your eyes. I pray that you let me know and practice the right way of giving unto you that is to give in secret. I know that men cannot reward me for giving unto you, but you will reward me accordingly because you know the position of my heart and the depth of my pocket. Help me, dear Lord, in Jesus's name. Amen.

16 November

"A generous man will himself be blessed, for he shares his food with the poor" (Proverbs 22:9, NIV).

Prayer Point

I knew an old man that was a giver. Whenever he came by my house, brought lots of fruit and vegetables or he would give us money. There was never a moment where he would meet us and not give us anything. He also gave to people who were in serious need.

He was a generous man and the Word of God says that he who is generous will be blessed. The Holy Spirit has worked within you and is using you to feed the poor.

Whenever you have abundance, thank God because not everyone lives in abundance. Ask God to help you share some of your wealth or possessions with those less privileged. God has blessed you in order for you to be a blessing to others.

17 November

"If anyone has material possessions and sees his brother in need but has no pity on him, how can the love of God be in him? Dear children, let us not love with words or tongue but with actions and in truth" (1 John 3: 17-18, NIV).

Prayer Point

To be able to give someone in need, show your love with actions. You could have brothers and sisters born of the same parents that have not been blessed the same way. The people who are blessed are not supposed to enjoy the blessings alone. When they see a brother in need, they should be able to help wherever possible.

God has a lot of expectations of the people who have been blessed with material possessions. Not only are they expected to give; they should also be in a position to identify a need and help accordingly.

God is love and everyone who believes in God should be able to demonstrate the love God has shown us through His Son Jesus. God has given you—and He expects you to give to the poor. When someone is hungry, feed him. God expects us to be His hands; if we give, we have allowed the light of God to shine to someone else through us.

18 November

"And do not forget to do good and to share with others, for with such sacrifices God is pleased" (Hebrews 13:16, NIV).

Prayer Point

When you share your blessings, possessions, or food, you can be sure that there won't be a waste of resources. Now and again, God presents us with different opportunities. These opportunities can make you successful. When you become successful, you are expected to share your success with others and get them inspired.

The things that God expects us to share are not always material; they can be in the form of good ideas that we have through the inspiration of the Holy Spirit. God does not want His children to live a selfish life; He expects us to sacrifice our time, skills, and resources for the benefit of other people.

God expects us to do good in whatever task we undertake—and be in a position to share how we got to accomplish some of our milestones so that others can be motivated. This is another form of giving—and such sharing pleases God. Pray that as the Holy Spirit inspires you, to share the inspiration with others.

19 November

"Command them to do good, to be rich in good deeds, and to be generous and willing to share" (1 Timothy 6:18, NIV).

Prayer Point

God expects us to gain rich deeds. God expects us to share because there are likely to be other people who will be inspired by some of our good deeds and they may want to follow into our footsteps.

When God has blessed you with the gift to teach His Word or run the administration of the church in a prosperous way, He does not expect us to use it for our benefit. God expects us to be generous when it comes to sharing the knowledge with others who are willing to learn. A major concern in certain churches today is that people don't want to share information or ideas because they want to be the source of information or ideas. As children of God, God expects us to share because we become rich in good deeds and God will bless us more when we share.

Allow the Holy Spirit to lead you to open up to others who may need knowledge through your good works—so that you may be open to share ideas and knowledge for the benefit of God's Kingdom.

20 November

"And my God will meet all your needs according to his glorious riches in Christ Jesus" (Philippians 4:19, NIV).

Prayer Point

If we could list the needs of each person in the world, the list would be impossible to go through. Although we may not know the kind of needs people have, we know that for as long as we live, we will always have needs.

There are needs that other people can help us meet—such as the provision for food—and there are other needs that no man can meet. Spiritual needs such as deliverance can only be met by God.

As you pray today, identify special needs in life that you need God to meet. Share the things that God has blessed you with.

21 November

"He who has been stealing must steal no longer, but must work, doing something useful with his own hands, that he may have something to share with those in need" (Ephesians 4:28, NIV).

Prayer Point

This verse shows that God expects each and every person to give or share something with others. There is something that each and every one of us has that God has uniquely blessed us with. He expects us to give and not withhold the blessings.

To steal is not godly; with the energy and wisdom that a person can use to steal, that person can surely be able to use that wisdom and the energy to do something constructive. This will benefit many people— even those who are incapable of doing something for themselves.

Pray that God helps you to generate income so that you can be in a position to share with other people who are in need. God prohibits stealing, but He encourages hard work so that the fruits can be shared.

22 November

"Whoever gives to the poor will lack nothing, but those who close their eyes to poverty will be cursed" (Proverbs 28:27, NLT).

God expects all of us to give to people in need. The world has so many people who have different needs. Some people are poor because they are physically challenged and cannot do things for themselves. Others are poor because of where they live. There are wars happening that are forcing people to run from one place to the other. No matter the difference in our social statuses, we are expected to give to those in need. It is something that anyone can give and it does not have to be in monetary terms or anything quantitative. You can give an hour of your time in a month to spend time with the orphans or you could go teach poor people in underdeveloped places to give them basic business skills to earn a living. You could share some of your groceries with the street children once a month. There is so much to give; as you do that, God will bless you.

The Word of God is clear that whoever gives to the poor will never lack. Giving is a sign that you don't merely exist. You are living and it shows a flow of blessings into and out of your life. God has given us so many things—not just for you to enjoy. He wants to use you as a blessing to other people. I know some people feel they can't give because they have worked so hard for everything and think that everyone should work as hard to earn what they have. There is no way that we can work hard without God's help. We have all these blessings because God has blessed us and He expects us to bless others.

Proverbs 11:24-25 says that one man gives freely, yet gains even more; another withholds unduly, but comes to poverty. A generous man will prosper; he who refreshes others will be refreshed. When you know that somewhere in your life you will need God to bless you, you need to start living a life that will be a blessing to others.

Proverbs was written by King Solomon who is known for his wisdom. He was rich, but he knew the importance of giving. He knew the consequences of shutting our eyes of compassion from the poor.

Prayer of the Day

Dear God, show me the opportunities that will enable me to be a blessing to others. Let my eyes and heart open to see the needy and be in a position to assist them. From today, I refuse to be like the Dead Sea where nothing lives. I choose to be like the Sea of Galilee that lives and that gives life. Let me be your light to the poor by giving anything that will be of value to them so that your name will be glorified. In Jesus's name. Amen!

23 November

"And he answered them, 'Whoever has two tunics is to share with him who has none, and whoever has food is to do likewise'" (Luke 3:11).

Prayer Point

Jesus emphasised the importance of sharing; anyone who lives in abundance of certain things that others do not have should be in a position to share. When you have food and someone has none; the food must be shared because we are all God's children.

Let the Holy Spirit prepare your mind to be always in the space to share with others where you have an abundance of possessions to share. Whenever there is an abundance of food, be prepared to share with those who do not have.

If you have too many clothes that you don't need, share with others who may not have. Schedule a time in a year where you select the clothes you don't wear and give them to others. Pray that God helps you meet the needs of others wherever you can so that He can meet your needs too. "If you help the poor, you are lending to the Lord—and he will repay you!" (Proverbs 19:17).

24 November

"He who oppresses the poor shows contempt for their Maker, but whoever is kind to the needy honours God" (Proverbs 14:31, NIV).

Prayer Point

God is our Father and Creator. He made us all—men and women, rich and poor. He had a purpose for all of us. The Word of God cautions us that we need to love one another, despite our social statuses in our communities because we were all created by God in His image.

The Word of God says that anyone who oppressors the poor shows dislike to God. However, the one who shows kindness to the needy is honoured by God because that person understands that we are all made by God and we are loved by Him no matter our social statuses or family backgrounds.

"The King will reply, 'I tell you the truth, whatever you did for one of the least of these brothers of mine, you did for me" (Matthew 25:40). God notes any kindness we show to the poor.

God's aim is to have us prosperous and rich so that we can be His hands and give to those in need. Pray that God can use you to show kindness to the people in need.

25 November

"Give to everyone who asks you, and if anyone takes what belongs to you, do not demand it back" (Luke 6:30, NIV).

Prayer Point

God expects us to help other people who come to us seeking our help and we are in position to assist. You don't need to know a person to be in a position to help them—and you don't need to have a lot in order to give. The little that you can afford to give matters. The Word of God says we ought to give in order to be given (Luke 6:38).

Pray for guidance from the Holy Spirit that you may be able to give to whoever asks anything from you. When something has been forcefully taken away, pray that God restores your lost item in the manner He deems best.

God is in control and knows how to punish anyone who forcefully takes away things from us. God knows the right punishment to apply when we are violated or have been stolen from. He has the power to replace what has been taken away from us.

26 November

"Bring the whole tithe into the storehouse, so that there may be food in My house, and test Me now in this," says the Lord of hosts, "if I will not open for you the windows of heaven and pour out for you a blessing until it overflows" (Malachi 3:10, NASV).

Prayer Point

There is one place where God is asking us to test Him—and that is to test Him with our tithes and offering and see if He cannot open the windows of heaven and pour out blessings until the blessings overflow.

God is a faithful God; He does not say one thing and do the other. He always sticks to His Word and never deviates from it. He is giving you an opportunity to test Him with what you have and to see if He cannot bless you and multiply your blessings.

The Church requires money, people, processes, and many other resources to function. Just as you have a house to stay in, a place where God is worshipped needs to be presentable. If you have not been consistently giving to God, make this season a time to start doing that and expect God's blessing to overflow.

27 November

"Share with God's people who are in need. Practice hospitality" (Romans 12:13, NIV).

Prayer Point

Matthew 5:42 commands us to give to anyone who asks and not refuse to help those who want to borrow. The scripture is encouraging us to give and share with anyone who needs something at that time.

The Word of God says we should share with God's people who are in need and make them feel important since they are important in God's eyes. We should also do unto others what we would like them do unto us (Luke 6:31).

Ask the Holy Spirit to help you practice kindness and hospitality—even to people you do not know. Always identify an opportunity to share any good thing with others since God has made us all with the purpose to love each other and look after one another.

28 November

"Give, and it will be given to you. A good measure, pressed down, shaken together and running over, will be poured into your lap. For with the measure you use, it will be measured to you" (Luke 6:38, NIV).

Prayer Point

When you give, you are in a better position to receive because your hands remain empty after you have given and you are free to receive. When you don't give, you have no room to receive because your hands are full already.

Giving is about an outflow of resources so that there can be an inflow. Without something going out, the place will be saturated and not have the space to receive other things. If you give sparingly, sparingly you will receive. If you reap generously, generously you will receive.

Start a season of generosity in your life so that God can return and multiply all the things that you have blessed others with. The Word of God says that it will be measured back to you by your standard measure.

29 November

"It is good to give thanks to the Lord, to sing praises to the Most High" (Psalms 92:1, NLT).

Prayer Point

It surely is the best thing to say thank you unto God for all the good things that He has done and the things that He constantly provides for us. There are things that God freely gives to us even though we may take them for granted because of His nature to give generously.

We may not know when we will die, but what we know is that God has blessed us with life. God blesses everyone with the air and the sun and nature, but we often forget to thank Him for those things.

Learn to thank God for all the things that He has generously given you for your enjoyment. Dedicate a period where you simply thank God for His provision and for His protection upon your life.

30 November

"And Jesus took the loaves; and when he had given thanks, he distributed to the disciples, and the disciples to them that were set down; and likewise of the fishes as much as they would" (John 6:11, KJV).

Prayer Point

Jesus was a busy man on earth; even with His busy schedule, He never ran out of the time to pray. He never allowed the excitement of seeing food before Him get in His way of thanking God for the provision before He could eat.

The things that God does for us daily are worth a thank you to God almost every moment. Even though we may fail to thank God every moment, why can't we at least thank God for something He has done for us each day? We should never allow the things that we go through to overshadow the blessings and provisions from God.

Thank God for your life, your health, your past, and your present. Thank God for the things that are still coming your way. Thank God for His provision of nature and for the air that you breathe. Thank Him for the blood of Jesus and for His grace upon your life.

Chapter 12

Thank God for His Grace through Christ Jesus

1 December

"Finally, let no one cause me trouble, for I bear on my body the marks of Jesus" (Galatians 6:17, NIV).

Jesus's marks on his body bear a lot of significance in every Christian's life. The marks on Jesus's body symbolize the pain and suffering He endured to save us from sin. Jesus Christ has paid the price for us to get entitlement to a new life through Him.

When someone chooses to follow Jesus, they choose to have the marks that Jesus received on the cross. The marks that Jesus has on his body are the marks of victory. Jesus conquered death—the last challenge for the human race. Beyond death, one can either go to hell or heaven, but Christians work all our lives for eternity because of our faith in Christ.

When Paul said, Let no one cause Him trouble for he bore in His body the marks of Jesus, He knew the power that He possessed by being Christ's follower. He believed in the victory brought by Christ's resurrection.

Beloved, reclaim your position as Christ's follower for you are redeemed. Let no one cause you trouble because you are more than a conqueror. Let no one tell you that you are going to die because by the stripes of Jesus you are healed. Let no one tell you that you are a failure because you are victorious through Christ Jesus because you bear in you the marks of Jesus.

Prayer of the Day

Dear Lord, thank you for speaking to me today. Lord, I thank you for the blood and the marks of Jesus. I am healed. I am saved. I am more than a conqueror—and I'm victorious. Activate the power I have in Christ Jesus so that I can fully utilize it for your glory, in Jesus's name. Amen.

2 December

"And now, brethren, I commend you to God, and to the Word of his grace, that is able to build you up, and to give you an inheritance among all of them that are sanctified" (Acts 20:32, KJV).

Prayer Point

In Paul's farewell speech to the Ephesian elders, he was basically saying a prayer of dedication of the elders to God and to God's Word so that they may be built and encouraged in God's ways.

We have not been blessed with the same abilities—and that is why even being a talented athlete does not mean that your children will be athletes. If you dedicate your children to God and to God's Word, then you are dedicating your children to the source of all power and wisdom that will uncover their unique God-given abilities.

Pray for the Word of Grace to bear the fruit of grace through you and those around you. Refuse to lose the inheritance that has been given to you through Christ Jesus.

3 December

"For the grace of God has appeared, bringing salvation to all people. It trains us to renounce ungodly living and worldly passions so that we might live sensible, honest, and godly lives in the present age as we wait for the blessed hope and glorious appearance of our great God and Savior, Jesus the Messiah" (Titus 2:11-13, ISV).

Prayer Point

Grace is normally defined as undeserved favour. Grace has been given to us as Christians through Christ. The grace of God makes us prosper even when our own efforts would make us fail. It is through the grace of God that you find yourself living an active life because not everyone is able to live that kind of life. Some people are bedridden and cannot do anything by themselves.

The grace of God offers us many great benefits—the ability to control ourselves and not indulge on worldly passions—and it teaches us to have the ability to control our emotions so that we do not act based on bad emotions.

Make it your prayer that the grace of God may teach you self-control in areas that you have been struggling with—laziness or a prayerless life—and that it fills your heart with the ability to be in control of different circumstances.

4 December

"For we do not have a high priest who is unable to sympathize with our weaknesses, but we have one who has been tempted in every way, just as we are—yet was without sin. Let us then approach the throne of grace with confidence, so that we may receive mercy and find grace to help us in our time of need" (Hebrews 4:15-16).

Prayer Point

Lord Jesus came down to earth to have the experience of the life that we live in and to experience the trials and the tribulations that we go through. When He was on earth, He prayed and fasted in order to draw strength from God and to overcome temptation from the evil one. He knows how it feels to be tempted because He went through temptation but remained victorious.

When we pray to God for help, God is able to help us overcome by His grace. It is through the grace of God that we overcome even the most difficult situations. It is through his mercy that our sins are forgiven.

Pray in confidence, believing that God will grant you the grace and mercy that you need. It will be sufficient to help you in the times of need. Pray that the grace of God equips you with the necessary ammunition to overcome any weakness or challenges.

5 December

"For the law was given through Moses; grace and truth came through Jesus Christ" (John 1:17, NIV).

Prayer Point

God gave us the Ten Commandments through Moses. Those commandments constitute the law that God has given us and expects us to live by so that we can live a life of righteousness that demonstrates the fear that we have for the Lord.

God has given us the grace to be saved through Jesus Christ. Jesus Christ came and experienced hardships so that anyone who believes in Him can be saved from all the suffering from this world. Jesus is the way, the truth, and the life; no one can go through God the Father except by Jesus (John 14:6).

Thank God for the gift of grace and salvation through Jesus Christ. Praise God for the love and for revealing the truth so that you may walk in His ways and live a life of godliness.

6 December

"But because of His great love for us, God, who is rich in mercy, made us alive with Christ even when we were dead in transgressions—it is by grace you have been saved" (Ephesians 2:4–5, NIV).

Prayer Point

As we go through life as born-again children of God, we always have the responsibility to acknowledge the love of God in our lives for choosing us and saving us by His grace. Not everyone in the world is a born-again child of God; it is by His grace that we are saved.

We sin almost every day. If we could enter heaven through our own works, it would be difficult. Looking at the manner in that we get tempted to gossip, be dishonest, or have unclean thoughts, we could have a challenge to live a perfect life in a world that is so full of sin.

Pray that the mercies of God follow you wherever you go and for the grace of God to awaken those circumstances in your life that make your life dormant. Thank God for His grace that has saved you.

7 December

"Grace to all who love our Lord Jesus Christ with an undying love" (Ephesians 6:24, NIV).

Prayer Point

Is your love for the Lord never-ending? If your answer is yes, you need to know that your love will go through some tests to determine whether it is superficial or genuine. These tests are important because they determine how serious you are about your relationship with our Lord and Saviour.

Paul wished grace for all the saints who loved the Lord with undying love. He understood that when you have the grace of the Lord, you will manage to go through life and win different types of battles.

The grace of God becomes visible in situations where you are not in a position to do anything for yourself—you may be relying on God's grace to aid you. Make it your prayer that you can grow in your love of your Saviour Jesus and in the understanding of His purpose for your life.

8 December

"And the God of all grace, who called you to his eternal glory in Christ, after you have suffered a little while, will himself restore you and make you strong, firm, and steadfast" (1 Peter 5:10, NIV).

Did you know that you need the grace of God upon your life to overcome? The grace of God is sufficient to carry you through all the challenges on this earth. It is by the grace of God that we managed to go to school and are able to read and write. People in certain parts of the world cannot read or write. It is by the grace of God that you are alive because people die every minute due to natural and unnatural causes.

The essence of this scripture is to remind you that God is a gracious God and—no matter what challenge you are facing—God will restore you by His grace after you have suffered for a little while.

Suffering is meant to strengthen some weakness in you so that you can be strong and firm. Suffering is meant to make us mature into the things of God. Some people miss the point when it comes to having to suffer whilst being a Christian. They assume that when you are a child of God, you are not subject to suffering. It is a sad thing to see a born-again child of God rebel against God when trouble comes because of lack of understanding of what suffering means. God wants you to be stronger than ever before. God wants to test your faith in Him. God wants to elevate you in times of suffering or hardship. You must know that your circumstances will be unique all the time—and you won't need to compare yourself with anyone else. What you need to believe is that God will put an end to suffering through His grace. Beloved, instead of complaining about the things not going right in your life, ask for more grace. His grace is what you need to overcome.

Prayer of the Day

Dear Lord, thank you for assuring me of your love and grace. I believe that my struggles are for a little while, but your love and grace qualify me for eternity. Help me stay true to you and to remember you always. Allow me to float over all the challenges. I pray that all the situations that looked impossible in my life see me as an impossible Christian to defeat. Lord Jesus, I'm tired of running away from situations. I pray that trouble runs away from me. I pray that by your grace, I attract everything that I have lost along the way due to confusion and lack of focus in my mind. I know that in certain circumstances, I did not trust you enough, but I pray, Lord Jesus, for your strength and grace to fill up my entire being, in Jesus's name. Amen.

9 December

"For Christ died for sins once for all, the righteous for the unrighteous, to bring you to God. He was put to death in the body but made alive by the Spirit" (1 Peter 3:18).

Prayer Point

It is important to believe in Lord Jesus with an understanding of the sacrifice He made on the cross and what that sacrifice mean to us during these times. God saw that all mankind had sinned; in order to cleanse us from all unrighteousness, He needed someone who was clean to reverse the curse that was brought by the sin.

Sin would result in eternal death, but Jesus Christ became a sacrifice for us so that our sins could be forgiven and we could be brought back to God. Jesus went through a physical death, but He conquered death because He rose from the dead.

Pray for the strong connection that you have in Jesus to grow from strength to strength that you may be able to see His fullness of grace manifest in all areas of your life.

10 December

"For sin shall not be your master, because you are not under law, but under grace" (Romans 6:14).

Prayer Point

Accepting Jesus as your Lord and Saviour means you are beginning a new chapter of your life. The things that used to control you before—lust or any other worldly pleasures—do not have control over you because the Holy Spirit in you is greater than the spirit that is in the world (1 John 4:4).

Jesus came so that we could be saved by Him through grace. Grace entitles us to renewed strength, wisdom, and the ability to overcome our shortcomings that were ruling our lives before we received Him.

Pray that other people who are not saved may see the light of God through you and receive Jesus as their Lord and Saviour so that the grace of God can take control of their lives.

11 December

"For if, because of one man's trespass, death reigned through that one man, much more will those who receive the abundance of grace and the free gift of righteousness reign in life through the one man Jesus Christ" (Romans 5:17).

Prayer Point

When Adam disobeyed God by falling into temptation and disobeyed God's instruction, he gave away his freedom and power to live the life that God had predestined for him.

God was disappointed by Adam's disobedience and the fact that he was God's first creation. He was supposed to have been a good role model for all mankind, but he sinned before God.

One man sinned and Jesus Christ came down to cancel the curse brought by Adam and saved us. The sin of Adam made everyone guilty of sin. Through Christ Jesus, we received grace through forgiveness of sins. Pray that God may use you to win more souls that will accept Jesus. He bore all our sins and suffering so that we could receive God's pardon and become new creatures.

12 December

"To keep me from becoming conceited because of these surpassingly great revelations, there was given me a thorn in my flesh, a messenger of Satan, to torment me. Three times I pleaded with the Lord to take it away from me. But he said to me, 'My grace is sufficient for you, for my power is made perfect in weakness.' Therefore I will boast all the more gladly about my weaknesses, so that Christ's power may rest on me. That is why, for Christ's sake, I delight in weaknesses, in insults, in hardships, in persecutions, in difficulties. For when I am weak, then I am strong" (2 Corinthians 12:7-10).

Prayer Point

I knew a woman who was happily married with children. In midlife, she got ill and was confined to a wheelchair. She was a born-again child of God who loved God so much and she prayed so hard for God to help her walk again, but she did not get healed and passed away.

This made me realise that circumstances in our lives can change at any time. Even when they change, God's grace will be there to take care of your needs. Despite her condition, she managed to send her children to school—and two of her children were employed at the time of her passing. Although she did not have the ability to walk or do things around the house for herself, God's grace was sufficient to raise her kids until they could be independent. God never took her before the kids were independent; He took her when the kids were grown up and capable of looking after themselves.

There could a certain thorn in your life that has presented itself in a form of financial lack, irresponsible children, poor health, or other forms of discomfort. You could have prayed different types of prayers, but there has never been a transformation in terms of your expectations. Believe that God's grace is sufficient to see you through all those problems.

13 December

"What shall we say then? Shall we continue in sin, that grace may abound?" (Romans 6:1, NIV).

Prayer Point

Receiving the grace of God through Jesus does not mean that we have the freedom to live a life of sin with the view that we will always receive more grace to cover all of our inequities and sin. The scripture again says "What then? Shall we sin because we are not under law but under grace? By no means!" (Romans 6:15).

We have the responsibility to love God and obey His commands. When our minds have been set to loving God, we will shun everything that is displeasing to God and we will adopt an attitude of righteousness.

Pray that God directs your steps into living a righteous life. Aim for righteousness so that grace may increase. Pray for your family, friends, and anyone close to you to seek the Lord and to live a life that will be pleasing to God so that God's grace may abound upon their lives.

14 December

"But He gives us more grace. That is why Scripture says: God opposes the proud but gives grace to the humble" (James 4:6, NIV).

Prayer Point

Pride is an inward feeling that has an inflated sense of one's personal status. Proud people feel superior and they tend to belittle those around them. As Christians, we ought to maintain a humble attitude because pride leads to disgrace; wisdom comes with humility (Proverbs 11:2).

God opposes people who are proud, but He gives favour to people who show an understanding that they are not their own god. God is the ultimate creator of all things in heaven and on earth and beneath the earth.

Pray that you find favour in God's sight by living a life that honours God—a life of humility and respect. Pray that in all the achievements and the blessings that you receive, you acknowledge God and always attribute the blessings to His favour and not to your own strength and wisdom.

15 December

"No eye has seen, no ear has heard, no mind has conceived what God has prepared for those who love him" (Corinthians 2:9, NIV).

To love God is such a blessing. When you love God and you do as He expects of you, you move in the direction that God expects you to move. God is always willing and ready to bless those who love and obey His commands. This scripture tells you that there is nobody in heaven or on earth who can accurately imagine what God has prepared for those who love him. It is God's secret! Wouldn't you be excited to know what is ultimately awaiting you that has been prepared by God.

It is so uplifting to know that it is God's secret that He only wants to reveal to you. This is one of those verses in the Bible that brings a spark every time I read it because it's telling me about the great things that await us.

It can be difficult to live in anticipation of good things if you have gone through many setbacks in life. You could have lost every single possession on earth—even your loved ones—but I want to encourage you to never stop loving your creator. One thing that is certain is that God has not forgotten about you. He is preparing something that is special that no one has had the privilege to see except for God.

This verse brings so much comfort because it reveals to us that setbacks are temporary and we should view them as that. After reading this scripture, be optimistic about the future, knowing that for as long as you keep your focus on loving God, He will carry you. Keep the faith and continue obeying God's commands. He is preparing something great for you.

Prayer of the Day

Dear God, I thank you for your love. I thank you for making it possible for me to be your child, Lord. Help me to love you unconditionally. Teach me to sing songs of praise even when the sun does not seem to shine my way. Help me to stay true to your Word and to obey your commands, in Jesus' name. Amen.

16 December

"Therefore, as God's chosen people, holy and dearly loved, clothe yourselves with compassion, kindness, humility, gentleness and patience" (Colossians 3:12, NIV).

Prayer Point

A true believer is not seen by what they say but is seen by the way they live their lives. As a believer in Christ, the spirit in you will move you into a life of righteousness. The Holy Spirit will allow us to bear the fruits that will attest to the seed that has been planted in us.

The fruit of kindness, humility, compassion, gentleness, and patience—if demonstrated in your conduct—will reveal if the spirit in us is the spirit from God or not. Allow to be led by the Holy Spirit of God.

Pray that God restores every good attribute that you may have lost along the way. You may have been so disappointed in life that showing kindness to others does not come naturally anymore. You could have been made to feel inadequate so that your ability to remain humble has deteriorated. Pray that God helps you to live the life that He has predestined for His chosen people.

17 December

"Since we live by the Spirit, let us keep in step with the Spirit. Let us not become conceited, provoking and envying each other" (Galatians 5:25-26, NIV).

Prayer Point

Living by the spirit is to live in a manner that is pleasing to God and according to God's standards. When you are full of the spirit of God and living by it, you will understand that God created you to be who you are because He missed having someone like you around. With that understanding, you need to appreciate the person that God has created in you.

When you see other people getting blessed, celebrate their successes because that is what God has planned for their lives. God could be having a different plan for you. Even if you fail to drive the car that you think about all the time, He could have predestined your children and generations that come after to be blessed through you; they will own plants that manufacture aeroplanes. Beloved, the scripture reminds us to live by the spirit so that we don't become conceited, envying and provoking each other.

Pray for the Holy Spirit to help you overcome any feeling of inadequacy within you. Pray for the Holy Spirit to help you live and strive for peace and to open your heart to celebrate the successes of other people.

18 December

"If I must boast, I will boast of the things that show my weakness" (2 Corinthians 11:30, NIV).

Prayer Point

Proud people often boast of the things that they have or that they can do better than others. Boasting is normally done with the intention to make someone else feel inferior or inadequate.

The Apostle Paul had gone through many challenges in life and decided that if there was something that he should brag about in life, it should be His weaknesses. He knew that if he was perfect, there would be nothing that he would need from God. Through his weaknesses, God would demonstrate His power.

Many people brag about their strengths, but forget that their strength comes from God. I want to invite you today to thank God for your weaknesses. Believe that He will work through those weaknesses to bring glory to His name. Weaknesses are strengths in disguise.

19 December

"Let him who boasts boast in the Lord. For it is not the one who commends himself who is approved, but the one whom the Lord commends" (2 Corinthians 10:17-18, ESV).

Prayer Point

When we receive our blessings from God or we realize that God has blessed us with unique abilities, it can be easy to boast about our abilities and forget to thank God in the process. That is a mistake because no one can do anything without God's help. In everything we do, God must be glorified.

Paul is reminding believers that when we boast, let us boast in the Lord because we are who were are and we have what we have because God has allowed us to have those things. The one who is praised by the Lord is approved—not the one who praises himself.

Pray that God helps you give Him all the credit for your successes, the success of your family, and their unique abilities; it is by God that you have been blessed.

20 December

"For I say, through the grace given unto me, to every man that is among you, not to think of himself more highly than he ought to think; but to think soberly, according as God hath dealt to every man the measure of faith" (Romans 12:3, KJV).

Prayer Point

Humility enables one to live a life soberly. Do not think that you are more important than other people. A person who is humble puts someone else in the position of honour. In the case of us believers, God is who we should honour and thank at all times.

God expects us to live a life that will not get us exalted but the life that will exalt Him because He is ultimately the owner of everything that we possess.

Pray that you may approach others in humility, acknowledging the grace of God upon your life.

21 December

"Having then gifts differing according to the grace that is given to us, whether prophecy, let us prophesy according to the proportion of faith" (Romans 12:6, AKJV).

Prayer Point

Have you ever realised that God has uniquely blessed us with different gifts for His glory? Many musicians sing well, but they have different voices and styles of singing. Every artist sings according to the way that God has blessed them and allocated the gifts by His grace.

God's servants in a church don't teach the same way; they cannot be replaced or substituted because each one is unique. God has blessed every person with a gift that is unique according to His grace.

Pray that God may start using your unique gifts that have been given to you by his grace. Pray for His guidance that you may use the gift in proportion to your faith. Thank God for the person that He has made you to be in the body of Christ. It was not by your own works that you are fulfilling that role; it is by the Grace of God. His grace will take you to another level.

22 December

"But we also rejoice in our sufferings, because we know that suffering produces perseverance; perseverance, character; and character, hope. And hope does not disappoint us, because God has poured out his love into our hearts by the Holy Spirit, whom He has given us" (Romans 5:3-5, NIV).

This scripture requires a certain level of maturity to understand what it truly means. You need to have been around to be able to relate to what the scripture says. How possible do you think it is to rejoice in times of hardship? Would it look normal if you celebrated after being amputated, having one of your children killed, or being diagnosed with an incurable disease? I'm sure your answer would be no! The wisdom from this scripture is that when suffering comes our way, instead of us blaming God, we need to know the role that suffering plays in our lives. Without hardships, we would never grow.

A good and strong character is what God expects from us. I have a friend who is so strong in the Lord that there is no problem that I have shared that freaked her out. She has always been calm about life's challenges. Sometimes I ask myself what it took her to be so resilient because I know that what she encountered must have been so enormous to prepare her to handle all problems in such a mature and calm manner. When you have not witnessed the death of a loved one until you are old, your understanding may not compare to someone who has had that experience when they were young. Hardships make us more patient—and lead to a character that is strong and mature. With a strong character, you will have hope in all situations with the understanding that everything else shall pass on this earth; your responsibility is to persevere until the end. We need to exercise patience in afflictions (Romans 12:12) and be faithful in prayer.

Understanding the purpose of hardships comes through the Holy Spirit. The Holy Spirit does a lot of things that humans cannot do. He comforts us. He directs us to pray in tongues. He transforms our characters for the better. An example of character transformation through the Holy Spirit can be a troublesome person who liked yelling and shouting. Once the person finds Jesus and the Holy Spirit has filled their hearts, they become calm and sober and act in a peaceful, loving way. The Holy Spirit of God is there for our transformation.

Prayer of the Day

Heavenly Father, thank you for providing me with the Holy Spirit. I welcome Him to occupy every room in my heart. Let Him occupy and give me the strength and courage to cope with a stressful and demanding life. Let the Holy Spirit transform my understanding into the knowledge of you and understanding of every situation that I find myself in. In Jesus's name I pray. Amen.

23 December

"Do not deceive yourselves. If any one of you thinks he is wise by the standards of this age, he should become a fool so that he may become wise" (1 Corinthians 3:18, NIV).

Prayer Point

When you live a life of humility, you give God room to lift you up. If you think that your abilities and strengths are adequate and you don't need God, avoid that danger so that you can start working your way up again.

To be wise by the standards of this age is to live a life that disrespects God because God's standards are not defined by men. Beloved, pray for the Holy Spirit of God to lead you into a life that will be pleasing to God. Always refer to God as the Creator of the universe.

Pray that God reveals areas where you have gone astray and where you have been adopting the worldly standards and not His Word. Repent of your sins and ask for God's forgiveness so that you can start a new journey of living a life by God's standards.

24 December

"Sitting down, Jesus called the Twelve and said, 'If anyone wants to be first, he must be the last, and the servant of all'" (Mark 9:35, NIV).

Prayer Point

The standards that have been set in the world today are such that many people want to be in the position of honour than in the position to serve. In some churches, many people would like to be served instead of serving others.

Lord Jesus told His disciples that if they want to be first in God's kingdom, they must be willing to be the last and be servants to all. God's standards are contrary to the worldly standards that encourage being on top without having started by serving.

The Word of God is saying that if you want to be the first in God's kingdom, you must be willing to be a servant. When you are a servant, you are starting somewhere. Start with the basics and work your way up to becoming the first. Ask God to equip you with an attitude of a servant so that you can work your way up to the top—where He wants you to be.

25 December

"Live in harmony with one another. Do not be proud, but be willing to associate with people of low position. Do not be conceited" (Romans 12:16, NIV).

Prayer Point

When God has blessed people with wealth, it can be easy to fall into the temptation of using wealth as a measure of the types of people you need to associate with and the kind of invitations that you honour.

The scripture reminds us to acknowledge the grace of God upon our lives by striving for harmony with one another. God wants us to be humble so that He can lift us up. God does not bless us so that we can class ourselves and build walls through the wealth He has blessed us with. He wants us to use the wealth and other blessings to build more bridges to connect with the people around us.

Pray that God helps you pursue peace so that you can live in harmony with other people. Pray that you live a life of humility so that God can take you to the next level.

26 December

"He said to them, 'You are the ones who justify yourselves in the eyes of men, but God knows your hearts. What is highly valued among men is detestable in God's sight'" (Luke 16:15, NIV).

Prayer Point

Do you live your life to please other people or to please God? To live a life that is meant to please other people can be draining—and can cost you to always act the part of the person that God has not created you to be.

God wants you to live a life that is justifiable to Him because ultimately you will be responsible to God. Certain expectations—even from friends—can be detestable in God's sight.

To defeat any form of pressure from any direction of life, seek to hear from God's heart and do the things that God values. What men value can be detestable to God. May your heart be filled with the longing to do the things that will be pleasing to God.

27 December

"For whoever exalts himself will be humbled, and whoever humbles himself will be exalted" (Matthew 23:12, NIV).

Prayer Point

When you exalt yourself, you make yourself look important and you expect others to see you in high regard. You feel superior in many occasions and expect this to be felt by the people that you interact with.

A person who praises himself has a problem taking instruction or being in a position to serve—and often values giving instruction over serving. God is a jealous God and He wants His children to praise Him.

God despises those who exalt themselves and He humbles those who think they are better than everybody else. God looks in favour on those who humble themselves. He feels that they are in a better position to be elevated. Pray that God helps you to remain humble even after big accomplishments.

28 December

"'Has not my hand made all these things, and so they came into being?' declares the Lord. 'This is the one I esteem: he who is humble and contrite in spirit, and trembles at my word'" (Isaiah 66:2, NIV).

Prayer Point

God is interested on our character development so that we can mature and be like Christ in the way we conduct our lives. Jesus did many marvellous things on earth, but He never boasted about the power that He had. He never made anyone feel small in His presence. He empowered His disciples and taught them to pray and had them increase their faith.

You could inspire other people in so many ways—and avail yourself to others so that they can learn from you. When you are humble, you become approachable and that is the character that Christ had. Jesus was approachable—and that is why people felt comfortable asking Him for healing and to raise their loved ones from the dead.

God values a person who is humble and has a spirit of repentance and a fear of God. To be pleased by our actions, He needs to have seen how genuine our hearts are. May God's grace transform your thinking and your attitude to be like Christ so that you can continue being highly valued by God.

29 December

"For the law was given through Moses; grace and truth came through Jesus Christ" (John 1:17).

Prayer Point

God's expected the Children of Israel to show their love and respect to God by complying with the law that was given through Moses. They had to do as the law required; that was their way of showing love and respect for God's authority in their lives.

When Jesus came down and made the sacrifice on the cross, God was basically giving us grace through Jesus Christ. Whoever believes in Jesus will be saved; all we need is to believe in Jesus.

After you are saved, you continue your journey by living in righteousness under the guidance of the law that was given to Moses. If we kill, we will be in the same league as the devil who came to steal, kill, and destroy (John 10:10). May God help you live a truthful life.

30 December

"Of that salvation the prophets have enquired and searched diligently, who prophesied of the grace that should come unto you" (1 Peter 1:10, KJV).

Life would be difficult if we all had to live on the merit of our compliance to the law and nothing else. It would be difficult to live a life where there was no grace because it would mean that we had a direct measure of what we put in. Because of grace, we are able to get the things that we could never get based on our level of faithfulness to God.

Jesus is all that we need; through His grace, we have been set free. Through his grace, we are more than conquerors. The birth of the Messiah was prophesied in the Old Testament (Isaiah 9:6) because God wanted to reveal this matter to the prophets first. Pray that the grace of God carries you through in your life.

31 December

"But when he who had set me apart before I was born, and who called me by his grace" (Galatians 1:15).

Prayer Point

Grace refers to the favour that you and I receive through Jesus. We are where we are today—and are who we are—because of the grace of God. Not everyone is a Christian, but you are a Christian today because of the Grace of God

You were separated from your mother's womb and kept by God's love. To experience how gracious and loving God is, He made us find our true selves through Jesus.

God knew you before you were born and He knew where you would be today. He called you because of His love and grace through the blood of Jesus. By His grace, you will rise above any challenge through Christ Jesus who brings us victory.